MW00396030

Vibrational Medicine

"*Animal Healing & Vibrational Medicine* deserves to be read and its contents explored and tested by open-minded individuals interested in the process of healing."

—Bernie Siegel, M.D., author
Love, Medicine & Miracles and *Prescriptions for Living*

"How refreshing to read a book on a controversial mode of healing animals (and people) by someone who actually knows what she is talking about. Beyond the emotional fizz that so often accompanies this type of book, Sage Holloway shows from the first pages that she is a person who is in touch with the vibrational energies that are an unrealized part of our daily lives. I enjoyed this book very much, and for all those people who are open to a deepening of the expression of their lives, while helping and healing their animals, I thoroughly recommend it."

—Michael J. Roads, author of *Talking with Nature*
and *Journey into Nature*

"Quietly, gently, radically, Sage Holloway challenges the veterinary industry to open its mind and its heart to a whole new range and vocabulary of care-giving. Every human being who resides with, or has feelings for, a member of some other species would do well to become familiar with these 'alternative' insights into health. As an interspecies guide, it is absorbing. Whether one agrees with all of its assertions matters not, for the underlying love of all plants and animals that emerges from the book can only help to stop the cruelty that Homo sapiens has collectively, insanely inflicted on mother earth and all her precious progeny for thousands of years."

—Dr. Michael Tobias, author of *World War III: Population and the Biosphere at the End of the Millennium* and *A Vision of Nature: Traces of the Original World*

"An illuminating guide of holistic wisdom that is essential to survival as a species and a wake up call that speaks to the amnesia of mainstream consciousness. As humankind awakens to its own need for natural rhythm and seeks to heal the separation of body and soul . . . this sensitive book will serve as the map . . . a way for us to see the road back to being keepers of the Earth and all her living creatures. *Animal Healing And Vibrational Medicine* is a resonant voice of the Ancient Future . . . it is time to celebrate!"

—Springs Romano, Ph.D., *Powers That Be*

"For years I have utilized vibrational remedies with animals— wild and domestic. They are one of the most effective healing methods for work with wildlife. Sage Holloway's *Animal Healing and Vibrational Medicine* provides very practical and easy-to-follow guidelines for using vibrational remedies with the animal kingdom. Whether a professional healer, a pet owner or even a wildlife rehabilitator—you will benefit from this text. More importantly, the animals in your life will as well."

—Ted Andrews, author of *Animal-Speak* and *Animal-Wise*

"A beautifully presented and thoroughly researched book. The many aspects of vibrational healing are now demystified and available for the healing of animals everywhere."

—M. R., Boca Raton, FL

"I appreciate animals being seen in their wholeness. The detailed chakras and energy systems are so helpful in my work with animals."

—V. B., Loveland, CO

"The first of its kind, this book is a gift. It addresses animals as whole and conscious beings."

—J. L., Fort Collins, CO

"At last! This is the book we essence practitioners have been waiting for. We thank you and the animals thank you!"

—K. S., CO

Animal Healing
and
Vibrational Medicine

SAGE HOLLOWAY

with foreword by SHARON CALLAHAN
illustrations by SAGE HOLLOWAY

Blue Dolphin Publishing

Published by Blue Dolphin Publishing, Inc.
P.O. Box 8, Nevada City, CA 95959
Orders: 1-800-643-0765
Web: www.bluedolphinpublishing.com

ISBN: 1-57733-078-1

Library of Congress Cataloging-in-Publication Data

Holloway, Sage, 1953–
    Animal healing and vibrational medicine / Sage Holloway ; with a
foreword by Sharon Callahan ; illustration by Sage Holloway.
        p.   cm.
    Includes bibliographical references.
    ISBN 1-57733-078-1
    1. Alternative veterinary medicine. 2. Vital force—Therapeutic use.
3. Vibration—Therapeutic use. I. Title.

SF745.5 .H66 2001
636.089'55—dc21

                                                            00-067499

    The information and material in this book is presented to assist
animals in the healing process. It is not intended to replace appropriate traditional veterinary care.

Illustrations: Sage Holloway
Cover design: Jeff Case

Printed in the United States of America

10   9   8   7   6   5   4   3   2   1

To Mother Gaia and all her beings of the animal realm
who bless our lives and grace our world with beauty, love and power,
this book is lovingly dedicated.
And also, to my wonderful daughters, Anja and Brittany.

Table of Contents

Table of Contents

Foreword

"It is only with the heart that one can see rightly.
What is essential, is invisible to the eye."
—Antoine de Saint-Exupery

A very wise teacher once said that humanity's destruction would come when its intellect grew while its connection to its heart diminished. This is what we have come close to. Our history with animals has been particularly dark. It is my belief however that, if we allow it to be, the new millennium, this new age, will be the age of the heart, the age of the return to essence.

The word "essence" as defined by Webster means "that by which a thing is what it is." Our salvation, the salvation of other creatures, and the salvation of Earth Herself will come as we return to our hearts, to our essence, as our source of wisdom and guidance. How better might we begin to develop our hearts than by re-establishing a loving, respectful and helpful relationship with animals: those creatures who have companioned us so faithfully for centuries, enduring hardship, loneliness, cruelty and often death at our expense.

Animals, unlike human beings, have not lost their telepathic link with one another. Each animal feels intimately the joy and suffering not only of other members of its species, but of all animals. Their ability to "feel with" one another transcends the confines of space and time, all events in all times merging simultaneously in the present moment. With this in mind, and reflecting upon the millions and millions of animals that have suffered experimentation, slaughter, cruelty and euthanasia over the millennia, we can then understand why so many animals experience anxiety and fear that to us seems to have no logical cause. Often, animals don't feel safe in the world even when raised and cared for by loving people. This is so, because they come into the world trailing a negative inheritance that we humans are responsible for investing them with. As an example of this, many animals are deeply traumatized by medical tests and procedures performed on them with the best intentions. These kinds of procedures stir in them terror of an intensity that we cannot even begin to imagine.

As an animal communicator specialist and flower essence researcher, the consequence of this kind of collective trauma and shock on individual animals is something I deal with on a daily basis. I consider it to be the major impediment to the physical, emotional and spiritual well-being of animals. *It is my belief that the first thing we must do to restore health and well-being to the animals is to ask their forgiveness and then to take the responsibility of remaining worthy of that forgiveness in our daily lives to the best of our ability.*

Vibrational remedies are the perfect vehicles to help us in this process, working as they do on the level of the soul, shifting consciousness, touching past, present, and future at once. Such therapies offer a gentle, non-invasive means of assisting animals in the release of past trauma on both a personal and collective level, bringing them fully and safely into present time undamaged and whole. This is where they can begin to fully experience our love for them. In this way, vibrational remedies have the capacity to act as sacraments of forgiveness between our species and theirs—the animals are set free from the shadow of the past, and we are set free also, to evolve and grow in compassion and loving kindness.

Vibrational remedies have the power to eliminate fear and anxiety that masquerade as physical illness in animals. When more invasive procedures are necessary to restore an animal to health to save its life, the use of vibrational remedies prepares them to receive such treatments in a relaxed and un-traumatized state, greatly facilitating both the procedure itself and the animal's recovery from such a procedure. For this reason, vibrational remedies are a perfect compliment to both holistic and allopathic treatment. More importantly, however, the use of vibrational remedies offers us a way to make amends for all that has gone before in the way of animal suffering.

Healing plants, gemstones, the elements of nature and the unseen beings who watch over each of these areas give of themselves freely and joyously for the betterment of animals, human beings and the Earth. In so doing, they are fulfilling the very purpose for which God intended them. When engaging all of the realms of nature in healing, we put in motion an infinite chain of reciprocity from which all benefit. In this way, each aspect is uplifted and exalted.

In nature, animals instinctively seek out the healing vibrations of plants, minerals, wind, water, sunlight, moonlight, and starlight to balance and heal themselves. Through domestication, cats, dogs and other animals are often deprived of contact with nature and those elements that would heal, nurture, and restore them. This fact alone is responsible for much of the physical and emotional suffering of animals. In addition, domestic animals are at the mercy of the inner and outer environments that they share with us, and are often totally dependent on us for healing and rebalancing. Because most of us lead busy lives and cannot offer our animal companions a life of intimate contact with nature, what we can do is to offer them the healing vibrations of nature in the form of tinctures, essences, and elixirs made from natural elements. In this way they are soothed and rebalanced in ways which are familiar, natural, and unthreatening to them.

Human beings ruminate over things, doubting and questioning in ways that prevent or lessen the effects of many subtle and even grosser therapies. Animals don't do this. They simply and spontaneously rise in consciousness to the highest vibration that is presented to them. Because of this, vibrational remedies often work wonders with even the most seriously traumatized animals.

In my own life, I have chosen the use of vibrational remedies, particularly flower essences, to augment my healing work with animals. I feel that their use is compatible with true spiritual healing which concerns itself not with the state of the body, or even ultimately whether the body lives or dies. Spiritual healing simply lifts the spirit into a state of grace from which it can choose the highest and best for itself. If the soul of any being is restored to its pristine grace-filled state, the body will function as best and as long as it can. If the soul then passes from this plane of experience, it can do so with effortlessness, fearlessness, and grace, achieving the highest state possible according to its individual capacity.

Over the years in my practice, I have seen hundreds of abused, neglected, and damaged animals restored and uplifted with the use of flower essences alone. Many people have reported witnessing a tangible change of expression, body posture and mood in abused and frightened animals within moments of administering flower essences. For those of us who love animals and want to improve their well-being, I can think of no better way than with flower essences and other appropriate vibrational remedies. In the process of healing the animals, we too are healed, our sacred relationship with all of nature is restored, and all creation experiences a state of grace.

During a near-death experience in 1985, as I journeyed to the "other side," I was not greeted by deceased relatives, angels, beings of light or even God Itself, but by animals. It was the animals who guided me gently and lovingly through my life review, and at the conclusion presented me with a vision of the world in its exalted state, free of the distortion of the human mind ... a world of peace, equanimity and the oneness of all creatures. I was told that the vision I was witnessing could be realized only if human beings became able to humble themselves and awaken to the sacredness and godliness of every living creature. The animals showed me that in the next few years it would become critical to feel safe and loved in the world, for without feeling safe and loved it would be impossible for them to perform the critical role they play in the unfoldment of consciousness. As a consequence, they said not only would they continue to suffer, but all of life would be damaged beyond its ability to recover.

The book you are holding in your hands is a timely and beautiful contribution, not only to the redemption of the animal/human relationship, but to the future of the Earth Herself. I suspect that coming into publication as it has at the dawning of the millennium is no coincidence. Although at times my own experience and research draw different conclusions to those presented in these pages, it is important to remember that the field of vibrational healing has only relatively recently undergone rebirth. There is much to learn and to share as we proceed. Working with natural remedies is a co-creative process with nature, and each individual brings their own particular perspective and energy, which is just as it should be.

It is of utmost importance to remember that Love above all else is the supreme healer. This book is filled with love. If used with the guidance of your heart and your own innate wisdom, the information included here offers tools to make the vision I was given during my near-death experience a reality. Combined with attention to our personal growth and unfoldment, vibrational remedies have the potential of restoring to animals the inflow of grace which has been obscured from them by our own shadow. Let there be light, and love, and healing for the animal realm.

Sharon Callahan
Animal Communication Specialist
Anaflora Flower Essence Therapy for Animals

Acknowledgments

Ever since a not so little voice whispered in my ear to write this book, it has been a labor of love and delight. Every chapter has been written and guided by forces beyond myself. My deepest appreciation goes to this entire support team for allowing me to assist in this work.

I would like to thank my daughter Brittany, for her patience, love and understanding during the research and writing of this book, as well as the use of her computer! Also, much gratitude goes to Chaz Dewsbury for his tenacious assistance with the Autocad glyphs, symbols and grid artwork, as well as his friendship and humor. Deepest thanks to my daughter Anja for her eternal love and support. Sincerest gratitude to Paul Clemens, for the vision and faith to publish this work. Thank you Annie and Sierra, for teaching me who animals really are. To Sharon, sincerest appreciation for your beautiful foreword and quotes. Thanks to Richard Gerber for allowing me to use your quotes. The information given from Hilarion through Jon Fox, assisted me greatly with the dolphin chakras. Also, great appreciation to the pioneers of this field, from Paracelsus to Bach, the indigenous cultures as well as the essence researchers and developers all over the globe.

And lastly and very importantly, a big thank you to my dog Jake, a constant source of loving humor, perspective and blessing to my life.

Introduction

We exist in a vibrational universe. We literally breathe and live in a world of energy. Though what we see around us may seem massive and dense, it is just a small part of all that exists. Even our physical bodies may seem to be primarily flesh and bone, but we are far more than that. Behind every living thing, there is energy. All form originates as life-force. Energy creates the physical world, and is the very life that animates the forms of this world.

The longer I live, the more obvious it becomes that everything we experience comes to us as an attraction of frequency. We vibrate at a certain rate, and bring into our lives all that is of the same frequency. Who and what we truly are, what we are made of by the frequency that we choose to own and express, is what determines us. This is not only our internal character, but our very resonance with life or death.

Since the invention of Kirlian photography about fifty years ago, it is now possible to see the life-force of living things. From flower to human being, the radiant energy field can be seen in its full scope and spectrum. This has shown scientists, physicians and lay people alike that energy is a key component to life, and is as pervasive and perhaps even more dominant than the physicality of living things.

I first experienced vibrational medicines through flower essences, in the early 1980's. There wasn't very much information at that time. Hungry to understand what tinctures made out of energy could be, I learned all I could from the sources then available, particularly Dr. Edward Bach and the Gurudas material. It seemed so profoundly amazing, yet simple, that the life-force of a blooming flower could actually be captured in pure water, by the sun! I was equally delighted and surprised with the results. Their influence could be sensed immediately throughout my body, subtle yet powerful. I have found that the essences of nature do indeed heal all aspects of her creation. What perfect sense!

Since those early days of discovery in my life, the miracle and beauty of vibrational medicines continues to be a deepening passion. I have watched the family of vibrational remedies grow. Elixirs are currently being made from thousands of gems, minerals, metals and elements. They are drawn from stars, planets and suns from near and distant galaxies. Flower essences are now created all over the world, in all climates and terrains, from trees, cacti, moss, and blossoms. The very heart of nature is manifest in her vibrational remedy repertoire, and is available for the healing, growth, and spiritual unfoldment of all.

Perhaps the most exciting aspect of vibrational medicine today is its application to animals. Wild animals, farm animals, creatures in captivity, zoos and sanctuaries, and of course our beloved companion animals, have a special relationship with nature. The essences which come from Earth and star carry the same frequency as animals do, easily providing healing and upliftment. Animals haven't the blocks of rigid mindsets and stuck belief systems to get through that humans often do. Many times, all that they need is very subtle and gentle assistance.

The animals of this world serve us, provide for us, rescue us, feed and clothe us. Yet they cannot seek healing for themselves. It is up to us as their human caretakers to provide the loving care for them that they deserve. Animals are great beings, who have consciousness, keen mental and emotional facets, and deeply spiritual natures. They are beings with soul. Perhaps even more than humans, they are creatures of energy and frequency, attuned to dimensions beyond what we can yet understand. For this reason, vibrational medicines are among the most appropriate and effective healing modalities available for animals.

Energy and frequency also come through the world of light and color, sound and aroma and magnetic fields. With senses several times more acute than those of humans, animals can easily come out of pain, shock and trauma and into radiant health, when they are assisted with support that is born from the natural world.

My purpose in writing this book is to provide for animals, through their caretakers, a clear and easily referenced guide and explanation of vibrational medicine. It is time to take the guesswork and mystery out of essence application. The gifts of nature abound, and it is my pleasure to share them.

What Is Vibrational Medicine?

*"Behind every material object is an astral blueprint of colored light.
In the astral world everything is motion, everything is living."*
—Paramahansa Yogananda

Every living creature has a gift to share with all creation. Tremendous healing can come from a tree, inspiration through the wisps of a cloud. The ready ear, watchful eye and open heart can find the wisdom of nature everywhere.

Much of the magic of the natural world is not seen with the eye, but is experienced intuitively. Her regenerative power can profoundly affect our emotions and mental state. Being in a beautiful outdoor setting can lift the spirit and make us feel grounded, connected, and in our own natural rhythm. This is how healing and attunement are experienced energetically for all beings. Re-emerging now on Earth are technologies which capture the essences and frequency of nature and make them available for the upliftment and support of all living creatures.

Life is energy. All living things are predominantly energy, with the form being just a small part of us. The energetic field is the blueprint for every living thing, and all perfection, as well as disease, originates there. When the experience of health and wholeness begins to be seen as that which permeates our entire being, from energetic through the physical, we come closer to the understanding of how life works and resonates within us all.

Vibrational medicines are remedies and technologies which carry high-energy frequency. This frequency invites the individual's energetic field to resonate at this higher vibration. This balances and heals the energy system out through the physical body, integrating the whole being.

What is unique about vibrational healing modalities is their nature and how they work; which is with Source, rather than symptom. Traditional allopathic western medicine struggles with symptom (effect). Vibrational medicine resonates with Source (Cause). It does not resist or fight disease but aligns with the perfect design behind it.

An ancient gift from the wellspring of nature re-discovered in this century, is the magic of essences. These essences, or vibrational remedies, are elixirs which come from flowers, gems, minerals, elements, stars, and environmental sites. Being vibrational, they carry little or no physical properties. The energetic qualities are captured by forces of nature (sunlight, moonlight, wind, rain, etc.) and infused into pure water, where the frequency is stored. Instruments are used to track and isolate the essences from the elements, stars and climatic environment. (More specifics on the preparation of the various types of essences are explained in their individual chapters in Part One.) There are many companies preparing these essences all over the globe, and more surfacing all the time. As simple as the process is, hopefully the day will come when people everywhere will share the desire and inclination to make their own unique essences and blends.

Vibrational support from nature is also provided through aromatherapy, which carries the energetic qualities of plants and flowers through their aroma. Aromatherapy affects all aspects of being: physical, emotional, mental, and spiritual. There is, however, a hidden component that is recently being explored: the energetic impact of aromatherapy. Specific aromatherapy oils carry properties, when perceived by the olfactory system, that affect the finer qualities of being. Animals are particularly attuned to this aspect. These energetic properties affect the energy systems as well as the mental and emotional components, bringing upliftment and balance.

Another important field of vibrational medicine is sound frequency, which can support all aspects of being through tonal activation and pure note value. As creatures of frequency and vibration, animals easily balance and recalibrate on all levels when sound therapy is utilized. Sound is vibration, and when used to activate parts of the body that are ailing or out of balance, can restore harmony with rapid success. It is the simplest of therapies to administer.

The experience of working with vibrational remedies can be subtle to profound for human beings. With animals however, they often have immediate and significant effect. This is mostly because animals have not strayed as far as humans from their natural frequency and rhythm. Animals haven't the mental blocks for the remedies to work through, nor do they have great expectations. They are attuned.

The strength and power of frequency these healing systems of energy carry steps up one's entire vibration. The energetic field cannot resonate with the increased intensity without shedding the old. It becomes natural and delightful to evolve and grow with these tinctures of conscious support. Deeper understanding of hurts and blockages that have held old patterns in place rise into the light of consciousness to be released. Exactly how vibrational remedies work with animals is very much a mystery. We do know that working with the energetic remedies of nature aligns us, animal and human, with the underlying strata of all creation: the energy that manifests from Source. One becomes attuned to the unseen dimensions of support and influence, the heaven that creates the Earth, the substance behind and before the form.

Part One

Animals—The Inside Story

Animals
As Conscious Beings

*"...It is a dark and cold world we sit in if we will not open
the inward eye of the spirit to the inward flame of nature."*
—Gustav Theodore Fechner

Native people throughout time have deeply revered and respected their animal kin. They have understood that communion between cultures, nationalities and species is known through communication with others in *their* tongue, seeing them as equal and diverse beings. When each species is acknowledged and celebrated for its special voice, the animal realm and all of creation is recognized as one. Someday this will be understood in people's hearts as well as minds, leaving far behind a worldly culture of dominance, subservience and greed.

Monty Roberts, who is one of the people that the book *Horse Whisperer* was based on, demonstrates this by his honoring of the animal species. Siegfried and Roy, the master Las Vegas magicians, exemplify their love and respect of animals in their lives as well as their art. Through this pure love and discipline, they demonstrate the reality of true friendship between humans and animals on Earth. They are consciously and deliberately breaking the ancient destructive patterns of man's brutal dominance over the wild things of this world. Because of people who share this conscious awareness, the paradigm on Earth is shifting from fear to love in the deepest core of human understanding.

Animals function in and understand dimensions that are foreign to most humans. They can sense floods, earthquakes, tornadoes and other natural disasters long before sophisticated instruments are able to. Dogs are now being used by a few progressive physicians to diagnose cancer in the body. For human beings to feel we are the most intelligent of all creatures on Earth is ridiculous. Humankind has left little legacy of such wisdom and grace, when compared to any other forms of life. Entire species of animals have been erased from the planet, due to this speciest attitude of hatred and fear. The slaughter of wolves in North America and Europe, largely based on irrational beliefs, has nearly decimated a noble and community-oriented breed. The near-annihilation of cats in medieval Europe because of paranoid superstition also removed the essential predators of the rat population. Of course, this was the reason the bubonic plague took firm hold, as the rats were the carriers of the virus, and were free to breed unchecked. The effect that this massive genocide has had on the psyche of the feline species we can only begin to understand. Human attitudes and disciplinary methods, such as using painful choke collars on dogs and breaking the spirit of horses in order to ride them, show the profound fear and mistrust that people have of others. This lack of respect and honoring of other species shows nothing but dense ignorance. The disgraceful fact that animals are still extensively used in torturous research and testing shows the true lack of consciousness in the human species. Taking time to love and understand an animal, and letting that animal love us, can be a profound and deeply satisfying experience. Whether this be our own companion animal, or one we have come to know in a zoo, circus, sanctuary or aquarium, a relationship of deep intimacy is possible.

Humankind is remembering to relate to animals as sentient beings with soul. Jamie Sams, a Native American teacher and author, has opened many people's eyes to the spiritual nature of animals. Ted Andrews has also taught through his writings and workshops, of the gifts of wisdom that animals provide. The creatures of this world can teach us so many things: loyalty, unconditional love, tenacity, and the art of manifestation. Their presence in our lives can show us humor, priorities, compassion, and how to receive. If we just listen

4

and honor, we can commune with each other as conscious, divine beings. If the human species were able to collectively (and individually) soften to receive the love and wisdom of animals, life would be wonderfully different. How long have the animal creatures of this Earth waited for us to understand who they are? Perhaps they are ready and waiting to teach us, and to learn from us as well, if we only let them.

Stress and Human Responsibility

"The love for all living creatures is the most noble attribute of humans."
—Charles Darwin

Certainly, one of the key buzzwords for the nineties has become stress. Every individual feels it, deals with it, and is overpowered by it at at one time or another. As the pace of our busy lives increases, so does the intensity of stress in all of us.

Whose Stress is it?

The medical community is recognizing the deadly role that stress plays in the cause of illness. It is a major factor in the suppression of the immune system, creating susceptibility to disease. Frantic and demanding jobs, lifestyles and environmental disturbance all lead to and create stress. When we allow our emotions and mental state to be affected by the stressful factors in our worlds, we become sick, and our animals become sick with us.

Mental stress takes the form of worry. Humans are the only creatures on Earth who worry. Worry is a lack of emotional control and instinctive faith in the perfection of life's unfolding process. Chronic worry is a bad habit that severely stresses the body on all levels. Animals, who are incapable of worry, pick up the effects of it from their human family and internalize it in their bodies.

In treating stress-related disorders in animals that we share our lives with, we must first look honestly at ourselves. How is the stress that we are carrying affecting them? What is the quality of the

6

emotional environment of our home, that we live in and provide for others? Do we create an atmosphere of peace, joy and well being, where *all* can feel safe and comfortable? Do we vent inappropriately? Or do we hold our internal pressures like a time bomb? How much of our animal's stress comes from us?

Animals who are closely knit with their human families experience extreme stress when their humans do. The affects of serious illness, injury and divorce are felt keenly not only by people, but by our animal companions as well. Often, the disease and trauma that humans hold in their bodies manifests physically in their animal's bodies and behavior. If we, as human caretakers of our worlds, do not honestly face our fears and life challenges, and communicate our feelings about them to each other, we hold them imprisoned in our bodies. There they stay, under the lock and key of our emotions. Left unresolved, these feelings begin to break down the physical body, from the energetic matrix of the cells outward, until disharmony and disease ultimately manifest. The entire process has toxic impact on our environment, particularly at home where we relax and let down our guard. Companion animals that sleep with their human family can be extremely susceptible to the psychic discharge during dreamtime that is released by people with unresolved emotional issues. This potent negative energy is as pervasive and deadly to animals as poison is to humans. Until we face the source of stress in our lives and deal creatively with it, it will have negative impact on us, on our worlds, our families and our animals.

The importance of finding balance in our lives, where we are at peace with our worlds, is paramount. We owe it to ourselves and those we love to take care of our physical, inner and spiritual needs responsibly, so that our animals need not take on the stress overload. Quiet time alone with our animals nourishes our internal lives. This cultivates a quality of substance and energy that our companions enjoy. Here they may feel comfortable and at peace.

Emotional Causes of Stress

Animals are keenly sensitive to changes in their environment. A new home, the loss or addition of new family members (human or animal), and extreme weather and seasonal changes are just a few factors that can upset the most calm and happy pet. Though these influences are often short-lived, without loving support the ensuing stress can continue. Changes such as these can trigger hidden fears from unresolved prior issues, perhaps prompting behavior that is unusual or inappropriate. Animals can be feeling threatened that there may not be enough love to go around from their caregivers. Since the emotional and physical bodies of animals are so unified, this fear can suddenly manifest as disease.

Specialized training for Seeing Eye or hearing dogs, as well as search and rescue dogs can be very stressful for them on all levels. Obedience training can be difficult, particularly emotionally. It is so important for animals of all kinds to be able to play. Adequate space and chew ropes, rubber and stuffed toys, and fun things that each species of animal enjoys can help to lift stress, especially when in training and in service to humans. Also, vibrational remedies can provide the loving assurance that is lacking, to address the underlying negative emotions and traumatic memories that life changes can bring to the surface.

All methods of vibrational healing outlined in this book are excellent for easing stress. Aromatherapy can uplift and promote well being. Music and sound can soothe and attune animals to the profound peace of nature. There are many vibrational remedies that specialize in keeping a calm and stress-free environment for all life's creatures. See the specific remedies for stress in the cross-reference section.

The primary need in any animal's life is love. This is the key to health and well being for every living thing. This is the greatest gift we can give them. This is their true nourishment. Nothing can substitute for it.

Physical Causes of Stress

There are several physical causes of stress in animals in today's world. Though the primary focus of vibrational medicines is on the energetic bodies, without the essential physical needs being appropriately addressed, the energy systems will be compromised.

All animals, particularly those kept in houses, apartments and small yards, need regular exercise. This is the primary way they burn off tension and energetic imbalance. Even a brisk short walk once a day will help to keep you and your animal more relaxed.

Almost all processed pet foods on the market today are grown with toxic pesticides and fertilizers. Processing techniques and chemical additives can further compromise animal's immune systems and organs. Healthier foods are becoming more available for them, as well as an increasing number of excellent books on nutrition and food preparation. Tap water also has it's own hazards, and is becoming more and more unsafe to drink. One of the most unsafe chemicals present in tap water is chlorine, and many animals, especially those who are chemical sensitive, have an allergy to it. Filtered water is the best alternative.

Medical and surgical procedures can cause upset to animals in every way. The procedures themselves often violate the body's physical integrity and cause emotional pain. Medications, and their invasive administration, especially taken long-term, can weaken the body's systems and create imbalance.

Environmental toxins, both indoors and out, can pose serious long and short-term health hazards. Dangerous chemicals in yards, gardens, orchards and agricultural fields can be deadly for domestic and livestock animals. These toxic chemicals can enter the body through the eyes, ears, nose, mouth and skin as well as the feet. Chemicals used indoors, particularly in new carpets and paint, can severely suppress the immune system. For animals that are inside and have little or no fresh air, it can be much worse. Plant and insect sprays, as well as harsh cleaning products, should not be used around animals, and always with extreme caution and ample ventilation. Natural cleaning supplies and furnishings are increasingly available, and are an excellent alternative to traditional, harmful products. Many of them are also easy and inexpensive to make at home.

Energetic Causes of Stress

The Earth holds stress in her body just as people and animals do. Her energy fields can become imbalanced, particularly from traumatic events such as sites of war and loss of life, natural disasters from fire, floods and hurricanes, and toxic overload from waste and underground pollution. Hydrogen and nuclear bomb testing has taken its toll. Animals can feel this Earth-stress, and are easily influenced by it. There is a growing awareness in people that the Earth is a living Being, who carries toxins and imbalances, primarily because of human ignorance and greed. With this awareness comes the understanding that we humans can assist in the Earth's rebalancing and healing. Healing modalities for our planet are surfacing. Feng Shui, the ancient Chinese art of placement, works in concert with energy flow and the proper placement of objects, elements, plants and minerals. There are also dowsers, Earth acupuncturists and energy workers who charge and re-balance the energy fields and ley lines of the planet. Using special tools and techniques, they seek to realign energy flows and grid lines.

After a move to a new home, even after everyone has had time to settle into the new environment, animals (and people) can seem jumpy and out of sorts. Earth-stress may be the reason. Vibrational healing modalities can help all concerned, but sometimes a professional may need to be consulted.

Lastly, animals who are closely attuned with us may find it stressful to continue to support us when we are growing and spiritually accelerating faster than they can track. The rhythm of personal evolution is not always easy or graceful, and vibrational remedies are excellent ways of keeping the entire family in sync and unified.

Soul Loss

Oh then, Soul most beautiful among all the creatures,
So anxious to know the dwelling place of your Beloved
That you may go in quest of Her and be united with Her,
Now we are telling you that you yourself are Her dwelling...
Her secret chamber and hiding place.
　　　　　—Saint John of the Cross, *Spiritual Canticle*
　　　　　　　　　　　　　　　　　(changes mine)

The primary schism on Earth today, in all her species, is between the body and the soul. Through the soul, all creatures know Spirit. We have each individually and collectively lost the experience of oneness with this Spirit. All sorrow and pain comes from this void. Human beings carry this wound from many generations past, beyond conscious memory. The trauma memory however, speaks to us still, in our bodies, in the formative matter from the core of our cells. Animals have inherited this pain and trauma from their human caretakers for centuries. They have carried it in their bodies and the collective unconscious of their breed, creating the same schism between their body and soul.

The longing of the human heart to transcend the pain and once again know the Creator as oneself, is the catalyst that breaks the illusion of separation from the Divine. However, the soul loss that has occurred with animals, especially those that co-exist closely with people, is not so easily healed. Often, this deep schism in animal species has left their trust of humans compromised, and they are leery of the very intimacy that would heal them. This is the time when vibrational remedies can be most effective. In their powerful and non-invasive way, they can provide the support for the integration and stabilization of the body and soul.

11

What Causes Soul Loss?

Soul loss occurs because of severe trauma-related stress to an animal, most often during gestation, birth or early life. As the animal matures, the deep disconnection to their world increases, with waning life vitality and animation. Depending upon the strength of the energetic connection between body and soul (that which keeps both aspects functioning together in the most basic sense), the animal may be too divided and compromised to continue to live at all.

Soul Loss Symptoms and Behavior

Behavior patterns that exemplify soul loss vary according to species, but there are common symptoms. There is often disconnectedness to people and the environment. There can be emotional lethargy and a lack of groundedness. A deep sadness and emptiness can be sensed. They may sleep most of the time (more than is normal) and show little appetite for even the most delicious food. On the other hand, some animals may appear perpetually nervous and edgy, have trouble sleeping deeply, and show fear and distrust of even the slightest sounds and disturbances.

Physically, animals that are body/soul split can have coats without sheen. The eyes are often dull and convey little spark. The glow of health and well-being can be missing. They may have continual low-grade infections or colds, chronic illness or wounds that will not heal.

The Support of Vibrational Remedies

It is important to first find energetic support for any animal that is body/soul split **before** intensive therapies of any kind are given. This is because while an animal is split, no therapy or healing modality will have much effect or hold for long. In addition, there may not be a sound enough body to receive strong medical or energetic treatment. This schism must be healed before the fragmented symptoms can be addressed. Thereafter, the quickening of the physical, mental and emotional processes can be dramatic and immediate. The animal will seem much more relaxed, at peace and integrated. Sleep patterns will balance. Therapies will finally take affect. With all aspects of Being now unified, the animal can safely receive greater life-force. There are many vibrational remedies which help to **strengthen** the body to receive the soul, **fuse** the actual body and soul, and then **stabilize** the body and soul as a single unit. Please see the cross-reference for a list of the many essences available to assist these aspects of body/soul fusion.

Communing
with Animals

*"The degree to which we are able to discern the aspect of spirit
through the physical veil and to disconnect from mass consciousness
and to reconnect to our essential Self and to Spirit,
is the degree to which we will be able to communicate with other
forms of life. Whether the object of our communication be animal,
vegetable, mineral, nature spirits, angels, or the true self
of a human being, we can only have genuine communion
from a place of egolessness and spirit-centered awareness."*
—Sharon Callahan

Most human beings live primarily in the three dimensional
world, with little awareness of anything greater. Animals however,
live in many dimensions. They "see" energies, thought-forms, and
emotional substance in ways that humans could only imagine. What
would it mean to us, and to our animal companions, to begin to
commune and understand each other at these finer levels?

The intimate bonds that are shared between animal and human
often touch into the magical realms of communion. Many times
what prevents a consistent experience of this deeper communion is
the lack of confidence in our ability to do so. Doubt in ourselves and
the higher dimensions can prevent the very experience of them.

A course of vibrational remedies can greatly assist the process,
chosen from the chapter on "Essences Are For People, Too". To
begin to consciously commune with your animal companion, it is
important to provide a time and space that will be quiet and

14

undisturbed for both of you. Let your mind be still and open, letting all thoughts go to the background, and be receptive. Only touch or gaze directly into your animal's eyes if it seems appropriate, but be content to just be comfortable and close. Once calm and mentally still, allow your heart to be open and yielded. Tangibly feel the love and gratitude you have for your animal friend. Honor and respect this being who loves you and is devoted to you. Ask that you may communicate, Divine Being to Divine Being. Do you wish to transmit or to receive? Your animal may have something to say first. If so, have no preconception of what you will receive, just be open and unconditionally loving. Or, you may wish to start with a clear and simple message, a picture, surrounded with feelings of love. **Animals are beings of feeling perception.** You may want to communicate a supportive message during a time of separation or grief. You may have a question for her regarding her behavior. Or, there may be a message to convey a constructive change, where it would be wise to offer a positive image (such as happily staying at home, rather than wandering the neighborhood). Keep the message positive and simple, and full of feeling. Then, be empty and ready to receive.

Here's where being human can often get in the way. In order to *receive* the message, one needs to be open to whatever comes in, without translation or interpretation. It may not even be the answer to the question you asked. Feel the information or image that comes. You may even feel it in your body as an urge or idea or sensation. Be willing to be transparent, and your animal friend will take advantage of the open communication. But remember, it will be coming from her perspective. Animals are not human, after all! They carry the wisdom and intelligence of nature, the Earth, and the body, un- tainted by the intellect and self-active mind. Let the message come through with as little human filter as possible. Then, trust your information. An open heart and mind, set with clear intention to commune, can only bring accurate results. So remember, if you keep it simple, and open softly to receive, it will happen. Most likely, your animals may wonder what took you so long!

Animal communication can teach us a lot about ourselves. How well do we *listen*? Do we really hear what another is saying to us?

And, if we have the courage to ask the honest question, do we have what it takes to receive the answer without fear or judgement? How tuned in are we to the substance of feeling and symbol behind the words expressed and received? Finally, do we have an agenda that the information needs to support? Unconditional love cannot be known without respect, and these are the keys to true communion. When the lines are clear and the channels are open, who knows what richness and depth can be attained and shared between all of us.

Invocation
and Assistance

"The animals want to communicate with humans, but Wakan Tanka
does not intend that they shall do so directly—
humans must do the greater part in seeking an understanding."
—Native Sioux saying

The interface of form and energy is guided and orchestrated primarily by angels and spirits of nature. These entities oversee and assist all living beings in their evolution toward Spirit and attainment of balance on Earth. They hold safe the mysteries of the hidden realms, keeping them protected from those who would use them unwisely or irresponsibly. However, these guides of the essential qualities of nature long to hear our invocation of them, their names whispered in respect and earnest on the behalf of others. They cannot come to aid without our asking, but are ready and waiting for us when we do.

All vibrational medicines carry angelic presence, as it is part of their signature. The more that anyone, be it human or animal, utilizes them, the more obvious this becomes. When invoking assistance from the flower realm, for example, there is a specific deva that oversees that particular genus of flower. There are angelic entities responsible for the entire flower world, as well as all gems and minerals, stars, suns and planets. Sacred and powerful sites are also held safe by these spirits. These are great Beings of compassion and wisdom, which overlight the entire dimension of vibrational remedies. When we align with these presences and foundational energetic patterns of creation and evolution, we can accelerate the integrative healing process for all concerned. Our animals can only find health and peace if we, their caretakers, are finding it and expressing it as well. Asking for and receiving the love and guidance of Spirit through all of her angelic allies is our birthright. This is the true experience of the essence of nature, of Mother Goddess, as oneself.

In working with any energetic healing modality, invoking the assistance of angelic guides can be very beneficial to accelerate the healing process. All it takes is a genuineness of heart, and an attitude of respect. Below, I have listed the entities that I have worked with for several years, who provide focus and overview for the realms of nature and vibrational medicine. Their names are provided for you in the same current of love and supportive guidance that they offer to me and this world. The most wonderful part of attuning to and co-creating with the guides and angels of nature is how personal a process of communion it becomes. Each and every creature on Earth has an overlighting Being of protection, from the most magnificent of galaxies to the tiniest of flowers. Let the support team listed here serve as a guide and starting point only. Feel free to explore the vast dimension of angelic guidance on your own.

> ***Archangel Michael*** *provides supreme protection, clarification and sanctity.*
> ***Archangel Raphael*** *provides healing, integration and wholeness. Restores beauty into form.*
> ***Archangel Gabriel*** *assists in perfect expression of one's truest nature, particularly through the spoken and written word.*
> ***Archangel Ariel*** *is the overseer, guide and protector of nature and her creatures in all forms.*
> ***Henue*** *is the overlighting Being of all vibrational remedies.*
> ***Hilarion*** *is the overlighting Being of technological information.*
> ***Quan Yin*** *is the overlighting Being of the healing arts and manifestation of healing and abundance.*
> ***St. Francis of Assisi*** *is the guide and protector of nature and the animal realm.*

Invoke the angel's or guide's name three times, ask for assistance in whatever way is appropriate, and then genuinely thank them three times afterward.

I also find it helpful to create a special place in the home that keeps the intention alive and consciously focused. If it involves the healing of another, a picture of them is helpful. A candle and a few flowers, as well as incense or sage to burn for cleansing, are all that's needed. Each time I look at this altar space, I feel more centered, rejuvenated, and supported deep within. This sacred space is inviting for guides and helpers of the hidden realms to come forward for the blessing of others.

As human beings, we have the privilege and ability to invoke these Beings, not only for our own guidance and support, but for all creatures who live and depend on us to intercede for them.

Dolphins

Of all creatures living on the Earth, dolphins are perhaps the most intelligent. They have the largest brain in relationship to body size of any living thing. They are graceful, artful beings, who love to play and have a strong sense of family and community. Their wide range of acute senses is multi-dimensional.

Dolphins have been in service to humankind throughout time. They have rescued swimmers and sailors all over the world. During World War II, many soldiers were rescued from the shark-infested waters off the Florida Coast. They saved the lives of the drowning seamen and carried them safely to shore. In Mexico, physicians and dolphins have been working with children with neurological difficulties and emotional problems by sounding sonar frequencies into their craniums. Therapists have had great success in treating autistic and emotionally disturbed children with dolphins.

Dolphins enjoy swimming with human beings of all ages, and people have reported a tremendous sense of joy and well being in sharing the water with them. They have demonstrated remarkable ability in communication, understanding gestures, and actual sounding of some human words.

The dolphin species is very unique to encounter and study. They are strongly family oriented, and have a tangible sense of play and fun. They are compassionate and take excellent care of their young. Their family units are large and very strong. Dolphins communicate through sonar, which is a complex system of sounds and frequencies just beginning to be understood by researchers. This sonar pulse can be changed and recalibrated for different purposes that only dolphins can understand, and may be the underlying secret in their healing of others. The specific rhythm that the sonar pulse carries is transmitted through the cranium to entrain the brain waves of the brain damaged or compromised person to the dolphin's.

Dolphins communicate with each other with unique signature whistles, which scientists believe are the equivalent to their own individual names. There is also evidence to prove, in some dolphin species, that these individual signatures, or names, are derived from its mother's. With highly developed acoustic centers of the brain, as well as water conditions and qualities (salinity and density, for example) dolphins are able to communicate and sense sound direction under water for miles.

The true purpose of the dolphin species on Earth has only begun to be grasped by humans. Continued research and work in inter-special communication will bring this increasingly to light. Many animal communicators, psychics and channels have been bringing the message for decades that dolphins have special gifts of understanding and consciousness for the human species.

Horses

"You become responsible forever for what you have tamed."
—Antoine de Saint Exupery

Humankind has a debt to pay to horses. Horses, perhaps more than any other creature, have assisted in the evolution of humankind. Before humans understood the great gift that horses could provide of speed, mobility and travel, they were used as food. As time progressed, humans learned to harness their great power for work; as farm and work animals, and for hauling and travel. Their strength, intelligence, teamwork and speed soon became essential to the modern way of life. Even in today's high-tech era, the mean measure of power is still measured in horsepower.

An ancient breed, horses have lived freely on Earth for well over 50 million years. Their thousands of generations of freedom in the wild changed dramatically when introduced to human beings. This relationship between humans and horses has been a contest of will for eons. The gift of the horse to the human race has been freedom and power. In return, we have rewarded the noble breed with cruel dominion and incarceration. Breaking a horse, through the domination of will and breaking of the spirit, has claimed their soul and stolen their spark. Human beings have left a legacy of fear and abuse of power with every horse that has been broken from the wild.

Horses have been used in warfare and battles throughout human history. From the slaughter of the Crusades through the battles of the Roman Empire, to the countless wars on the North American continent, humans have led horses to their death.

Horses aid in rescue, law enforcement, and entertainment in shows and rodeos. Essential to many sports, such as polo, racing, and hunting, they are often shamefully discarded like worn property when past peak performance.

Horses carry a mystery and power that is seldom seen in any other creature. Majestic, massively strong and independent, they are also friendly, caring and social. Gentle and mellow, they can also express unbridled rage and ferocity. Beings of great sensitivity and heart, the ultimate pain a horse must endure is isolation. Horses are herd animals that must be in social interaction to be content. Close contact with their own species or other animal species is essential for their well being. Without this interaction, their need for close human contact is even more important.

Monty Roberts, who has written *The Man Who Listens to Horses,* intimately understands the horse psyche. He has learned to commune with the species through countless hours of observation of their postures and movements in the wild. By posturing to animals in the same way they do to each other, he has acquired the ability to literally understand and "speak" their language. Monty feels that there is evidence on Earth of a new attitude of respect, love and communion between people and animals. His example, along with many others like him, provides a new paradigm of inter-special communication, love and respect.

Dogs

"Give a dog a purpose, and he will shine."

—Jessica Dunn

Truly the best friend of humankind, the dog embodies loyalty, protection, and service. Throughout history, dogs have served the human family by protecting livestock, people and property, as guardians, hunters, trackers, fighters, law enforcers, sled dogs, and hearing and Seeing Eye dogs. The have rescued on land, in water and snow. Their very bodies have kept people alive, being used for warmth and even food. The depth of compassion in all canine breeds has provided comfort and ease to people of all cultures and nations throughout time.

An ancient breed, dogs descended from their early ancestors at least 25 million years ago. Members of the dog family (canids) live on every continent except Antarctica, and in almost every climate on Earth. They are unsurpassed in both endurance and adaptability, as they have survived in the wild and thrived in domestic life through-out the centuries.

Wild dogs, wolves, coyotes and foxes have been hunted for kill or bounty for centuries in North America. However, over time it has become apparent that an imbalance of nature has resulted in many geographical areas, as rodent populations have increased and de-stroyed vegetation essential for cattle and livestock. Many efforts are underway to restore wolves to their native habitat, through federal organizations and concerned private citizens.

Dogs love nature. They experience their bliss by running through fields and forests, along ocean beaches and through streams and rivers. They smell the air to discern hidden messages on the wind. They love to roll in the dirt and feel the sun on their bodies. For dogs who rarely get outside, this lack of communion with nature can compromise their well being. Vibrational medicines can provide wonderful assistance for them.

Of all domestic animals, dogs are the easiest to train. Unfortunately, the dog's pure and unconditionally loving nature can be easily taken advantage of. Inhumane disciplinary and teaching techniques involve violence, using fear and power to motivate and control. This history of dominance and abuse of what are perceived as "subservient" species by arrogant human beings, often backfires. Rottweillers, for instance, have been trained for centuries as extremely aggressive guard dogs. By the shaping and manipulation of their genetic code from love to fear, they have been known to attack children and family members without warning or provocation. Chronic, deep-seated fear breeds hatred, and continues to do so until the cycle is broken.

Because of the true unconditional love that dwells within the heart of every dog, they are particularly vulnerable to abuse. Dogs will continue to love and accept their caregivers, even if they jeopardize their lives and well being to do so. A dogs allegiance is unwavering, their trust constant.

As human beings and stewards of all life forms on Earth, we have the honor and responsibility to respect, love and learn from all other creatures. Dogs, who serve and love us completely, deserve no less than the same. The essences of nature provide special support for the healing, balance and upliftment of the canine family. These can be found in the cross-reference section under Dogs.

Cats

*"Thou art the Great Cat, the avenger of the gods, and the judge
of words, and the president of the sovereign chiefs and the governor
of the holy circle, thou art indeed ... the Great Cat."*
Inscription on the Royal Tomb of Thebes

Throughout history, cats have held a place of mystery and power. From "guardians of the underworld" to skilled predators of dangerous rodents, cats have played a vital role to human beings for thousands of years. They are creatures of the night who can never really be tamed. They have been feared, mistrusted and misunderstood, which has led to their near annihilation in times past.

The cat's night vision is excellent, as well as their peripheral and binocular (distance) vision. Feline hearing is ultra-sensitive, particularly to the ultrasonic range. If you want your cat to come to you, call him with high-pitched sounds, and he'll come running. The cat's sense of smell is equally keen, and male cats can smell a female in heat hundreds of yards away. Independent and instinctual, anyone who has ever "owned" a cat knows that quite the opposite is true, and indeed, we are lucky to be owned *by* a cat.

Felines are one of the only land species that hear and vocalize the hum and rhythm of the Planet. Their purring is not only a vocal display of contentment and pleasure, but is actually the audible rhythm of the Earth's pulse, which cats hear, access and vocalize. This can easily be felt when a cat lies on your body, and your entire being vibrates in rhythm to him and a deeper, more profound pulse. Cats can reestablish and balance your rhythm, and will often lie on top of you for that purpose.

Cats have a special relationship with nature and flowers. They love to walk in tall grasses and snooze in flowerbeds. Cats love direct sunshine, and can sleep in it for hours. And sleep they do, for at least eighteen hours a day, dwelling in the mysterious dreamtime more often than in the waking hours. Who knows what angelic spirits they commune with while they sleep? Or while they are awake? How many dimensions do they see into with their haunting, inquisitive eyes?

For cats who live indoors, have little or no direct sunlight or fresh air and cannot feel earth beneath their paws or the wind in their sweet faces, essences can be vital to every aspect of their health. Fresh flowers are important in the home, especially at their level, where they can smell them and feel them in their faces.

Whether it be a panther, tiger, lynx or Siamese, cats command respect. They live from their instinctual nature, creatures of depth and acumen. People have kept cats because of their keen perception and sensitivity. However, a cat's psychic nature is also extremely vulnerable to negativity, toxins on all levels from all sources, and upset from stress from their human and animal companions. Their ability to receive subtle information and inability to shield themselves from it, often results in their being bombarded by negative emotions, thought-forms and physical disease. Even in households where the atmosphere is relatively healthy, all of us at times face stress, crisis and loss, and we count on our animal companions to love us through these difficult times. Essences provide effective support and protection for this hypersensitive species.

As the frequency on Earth continues to step up, we humans are challenged to grow and expand to stay in rhythm with the Cosmos. For our feline companions, this task can be very challenging, as their highly-tuned energy systems go through frequency shift after shift to keep up with us. Once again, essences are excellent tools to uplift and recalibrate them, and to support and strengthen their being as they continue to provide so much for us.

Essences that are especially supportive of the feline family can be found in the cross-reference section under Cats.

Birds

"The music soars within the little lark, and the lark soars."
—Elizabeth Barrett Browning

Birds bring a special dimension of sound, beauty and power to this world. Their sweet voices can lift the spirits and brighten the darkest day.

Raptors in the wild have extremely acute senses, and are intelligent, wise and patient. Creatures of great stamina and strength, some bird species can fly for weeks at a time without stopping. Peregrine falcons can dive to the Earth at speeds over 200 miles an hour. Golden eagles, perhaps the most majestic, respected and powerful birds on Earth, are used to hunt wolves in Russia.

Many scientists believe that birds are actually dinosaurs in evolved form, and that they have been on Earth for millennia. Their faces and bodies have been carved in stone in ancient temples around the globe, honoring their keen vision and powers that come not just from this world. Because birds are creatures of the air, many indigenous peoples feel they have a special affinity with Spirit. Birds are harbingers to all living creatures of the soul's passage into birth and death. Humans can learn many things from these beings that dwell in many dimensions. Indigenous people feel the spirit of the bird is carried beyond death in their feathers, and use them as talismans and tools of power.

Wild birds can be rescued and nurtured until they can be re-released into the wild with little difficulty. Essences can be excellent for reducing shock and fear, and with patience and hand feeding, many birds are often able to thrive in the wild once again. Most wild birds will die in captivity if kept for long, and should be released as soon as possible.

Domesticated birds can be friendly, funny, affectionate and intelligent. Birds are excellent communicators, and can even be cuddly, and some say they have a sense of humor. They are loyal companions, require minimum care, and some larger species can live as long as humans. Easy to train when acquired young, they can be great fun and entertainment for the whole family. They are quite intelligent and enjoy humans immensely. Perhaps we humans provide entertainment for them, as well!

Specific vibrational remedies that work especially well with birds can be found under Birds in the cross-reference section.

Reptiles

Ancient and adaptable, reptiles are feared and often misunderstood by most people. However, anyone who has shared their life with a snake or toad, knows how affectionate, intelligent and primordial these creatures can be. Reptiles are very unique. Some species of reptiles can regenerate and adapt to the environment almost to the point of invisibility. They can lose part of their tails and grow them back. Some shed their entire skin during seasonal changes. They range in size from the tiny newt to Komodo dragons, alligators and crocodiles. The Komodo dragon is one of the most intelligent breeds of reptiles. Komodos can weigh 300 pounds and grow to over ten feet in length, and live over 100 years. They can run at speeds up to twelve miles an hour.

Reptiles embody the ancient wisdom and rhythm of early life on Earth. They are perhaps the most sensitive of all creatures to their environment. They can move with almost painful deliberation, or strike in a hundredth of a second. Reptiles are able to lie still for hours in the sun, or move great distances at lightning speed. Snakes will vibrate an almost purring sound through their bodies when being safely handled. They will sleep under another animal for warmth (and possibly affection) without their detection.

In captivity, a reptile's basic needs are few and easy to meet, and for this reason make excellent pets requiring little care. They can be entertaining for children and adults alike, and are among nature's most fascinating creatures.

Rodents

Though rodents are primarily considered to be unwanted pests, they have provided companionship and entertainment to people of all cultures for centuries. Rodents are mammals, and there are more species of rodents than any other mammalian order. Though their size can vary greatly, universally they have well-developed ears and hearing and live all over the world. Rodents are very adaptable, and have various habitats. Some are aquatic; others are land dwellers and live in underground burrows or in trees. Muskrats, beavers, groundhogs and marmots all have a strong sense of family and community, and share in family responsibility. They also have beautiful coats, which have been used for fur for hundreds of years and have driven many species to near extinction.

Gerbils, hamsters, guinea pigs, mice and rats are popular house pets. They have been known to bond with their humans, and can be very affectionate. Pet rodents can be gentle, sweet and easy to care for, and are ideal for small homes and apartments. They can be very entertaining for those who are housebound or convalescing. Many rodent species are meticulous as well as intelligent, and if acquired young enough, show unusual affection and warmth to their human companions. They are also quite trainable.

For those who are fortunate enough to have developed a rapport with the neighborhood squirrels, they can be terrific allies and a consistent source of joy and play. I once lived in a home with a huge cottonwood tree in the yard, which had been home to several generations of squirrels, all of whom trusted people enough to eat from our hands. It was an honor to have their trust and respect. Feeders full of nuts, seeds and fruits will attract these playful creatures to your yard. Essences to assist them in trusting humans or with illness can be placed in their food or a nearby birdbath. The birds won't mind—there's something in each essence for everyone!

Of all the domesticated creatures, rodents are among the most nature and light deprived. They have little or no contact with the sun, grasses, flowers, trees, and other animals, as well as fresh air. Vibrational remedies can be excellent for nature and light deprivation. Essences can be particularly useful for rodents for ease in transition when first acquired or with the addition of a new family member or move. Also, any stage of the birth process for mother or young can be assisted. Diseases such as parasites, cuts and skin damage, diarrhea and fur loss can be greatly alleviated with vibrational remedies. Essences especially good for rodents can be found in the cross-reference guide.

Fish

Few creatures on Earth display such color, variety and beauty as fish. They live in every aquatic habitat. Living in the coldest, deepest oceans to desert lakes and even hot springs, they are adaptive and resilient creatures. They have been on Earth for at least 450 million years, surviving massive climatic global change and epochs.

Fish are largely creatures of vibration. They hear through inner ears which pick up sound vibrations through the bones of the skull. They also have unique sensory organs that detect extremely low-frequency vibrations, and in some species, can sense weak electrical fields.

Fish have been admired as pets in households of royalty and paupers in all cultures throughout time. As simple as a goldfish in a small bowl to sharks in massive aquariums, these creatures have provided fascinating entertainment and relaxing calm to all who experience them. One of the most spectacular kinds of fish are koi. These are ornamental carp that can grow from five to eighty pounds and live for years. They will come to feed directly from the hand with a little patience.

Most fish require little care, but salt-water varieties can be delicate and time-consuming. Fish that live in aquariums with voltage devices (such as pumps, powerheads, etc.) have been known to experience health problems, such as lateral line disease, fin erosion and gill deterioration. A few quartz crystals in the bottom of the tank can help to energize the water and dispel negative energy from the water, especially with illness or death in the tank. Live plants are very beneficial also. In all cases of stress, disease, shock and transition, just a few drops of specific essences in the water can help tremendously. Essences that come from sea minerals (corals, for instance) and sea lettuce and kelps can greatly assist salt-water fish kept in tanks. For fresh water fish that are kept in tanks, essences from all water plants provide support. Remedies for fish can be found in the cross-reference section.

The Energetic Systems of Animals

"Medicine is at the threshold of discovering a hidden world of unseen energies that will help to diagnose and heal illness as well as allow researchers to gain new insights into the hidden potentials of consciousness. The etheric level of energy will be the first of these unseen worlds to be explored by enlightened scientists. Researchers will discover that the etheric body is an energetic growth template which guides the growth and development as well as the dysfunction and demise of all (human) beings. Based upon the evolved insights of these enlightened researchers, medicine will begin to comprehend that it is at the etheric level that many diseases have their origins."
—Richard Gerber, M.D., *Vibrational Medicine*
(parentheses added)

Animals have energy systems and energy centers as part of their bodies, just as people do. The energy centers are called chakras, the focal points that draw in and regulate the life-force energy of the physical body. Each chakra corresponds to an organ, and most specifically, to the endocrine gland in or near the organ.

Some animals have fewer chakras than humans. Each chakra varies in purpose, energy and intensity. When an energy center is out of balance by being either too open or too closed, the imbalance will be reflected in the corresponding part of the body. For instance, damage or imbalance in the throat chakra can manifest as throat pain or mouth and jaw problems.

35

Vibrational remedies are of the same frequency as these energy centers, and affect them profoundly. Energetic medicines are particularly attuned to the energetic matrix of all life, the invisible spirit and rhythm behind the form. The relationship of energy medicines and the body's energy systems is holographic in nature, and when joined can allow deep shifts and recalibrations that go beyond the linear comprehension of traditional medicine.

Understanding the basic function and qualities of our animal's chakra system can greatly aid our ability to help strengthen and realign their entire being. Weak organs and systems can be identified by the health or imbalance of the corresponding chakra. This can be very helpful in identifying the underlying cause of symptoms and disease.

To actually feel the energy of the animal's various chakras, it takes just a little practice and a few special moments once or twice a day. Holding your hands on each side of the animal's body at the chakra point is an excellent way to sense the energy. Your hands will begin to tingle and get warm. Each chakra has its own special quality and feel.

The chakra diagrams that follow are specific to the major animal species. In smaller animals, the chakras may be fewer but will carry qualities of energy that may cover larger areas of the body. For instance, in birds, the actual solar plexus chakra may carry energy of the belly chakra, but be focused in the solar plexus or liver area. There are certain blendings of energies that are not exactly the same for all species. The first chakra, for example, may have roughly the same characteristics in a lion and a fish, but will vary in frequency, quality and intensity, as well as color. The function, generally, is the same. Also, all chakra points are both in the front and back of body. For brevity, just the primary chakras on the body itself are listed. There are many more chakra points both above and below the body than are generally known, in all living creatures. The energetic healing systems outlined in this book address the primary chakras. The functions, qualities, corresponding notes and organs of each chakra are also listed. The corresponding colors for each chakra can be seen on the animal diagrams which follow. Unfortunately, the colors illustrated here are of the limited visual spectrum that we see with our physical eyes. Dolphins, for example, have chakra centers which vibrate from the infra-red to ultra-violet range, and many higher chakra centers in several species radiate colors that are nameless, which may be iridescent or translucent. The colors used here are very basic, but effective and accurate enough for working in attunement to the energy centers.

The diagrams of the individual animal's energy fields are very similar in all animal species: the physical body, the etheric body, the astral body, mental body and causal or spiritual bodies. These energy layers are in reality much "larger" and energetically dense than the physical body. Animals attract, relate to and repel each other through this keen energetic communion. They are part of larger soul groups, called oversouls, and are not individuated souls, as humans are. The largest part of an animal's energy field is the astral body (aura), which is profoundly connected to the oversoul of that particular animal species. Specific qualities and chakra relationships of the energy field are listed below and on the following page.

CHAKRA CHART

SYMBOL	#	NAME	COLOR	NOTE	ORGAN	QUALITY	ELEMENT
	1	ROOT	RED	C	SEXUAL ORGANS	VITAL	EARTH
	2	BELLY	ORANGE	D	SPLEEN	JOVIAL	WATER
	3	SOLAR PLEXUS	YELLOW	E	ADRENALS	SELF-CONFIDENT	FIRE
	4	HEART	GREEN	F(#)	HEART/THYMUS	FRIENDLY/DEVOTED	AIR
	5	THROAT	BLUE	G#	THYROID	CONTENT/PATIENT	ETHER
	6	BROW	INDIGO	A	PITUITARY	OBSERVANT AWARE	TRANS-CENDS
	7	CROWN	VIOLET/GOLD	B	PINEAL	WISE/PEACEFUL	TRANS-CENDS

ENERGY FIELD CHART

COLOR	LAYER	BODY	CHAKRA	QUALITY
Red	Physical Body/ Etheric Body	Physcial	Root	Life Energy
Orange	Astral	Emotional	Belly	Feeling Instinct
Yellow	Lower Mental	Mental	Solar Plexus	Mental Understanding
Green	Higher Mental	Mental	Heart	Intuition
Blue	Lower Spiritual	Spiritual	Throat	Will
Indigo	Middle Spiritual	Spiritual	Brow	Communion
Violet	Higher Spiritual	Spiritual	Crown	Service/Oneness

Energy Field &
Chakra Diagrams

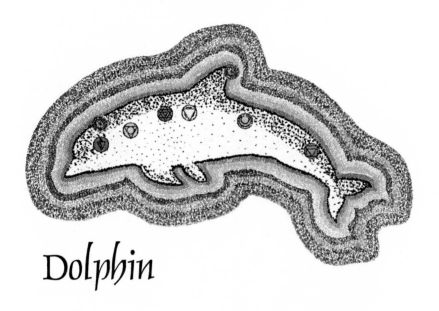

Dolphin

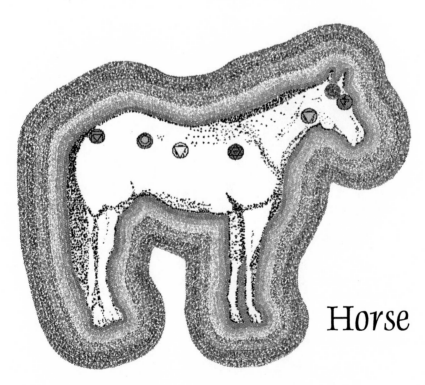

Horse

Cat

Dog

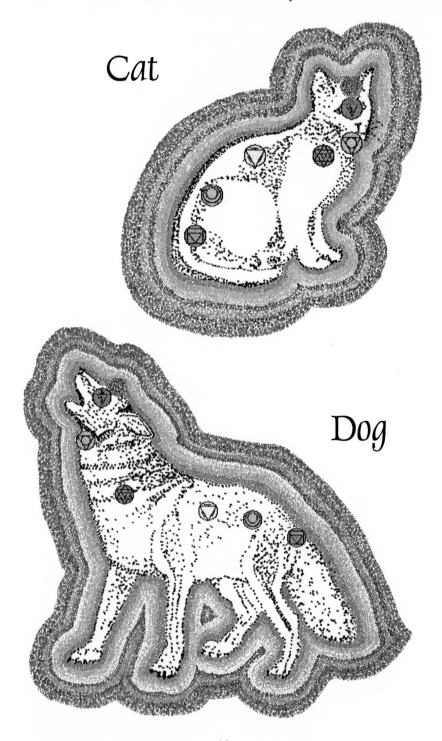

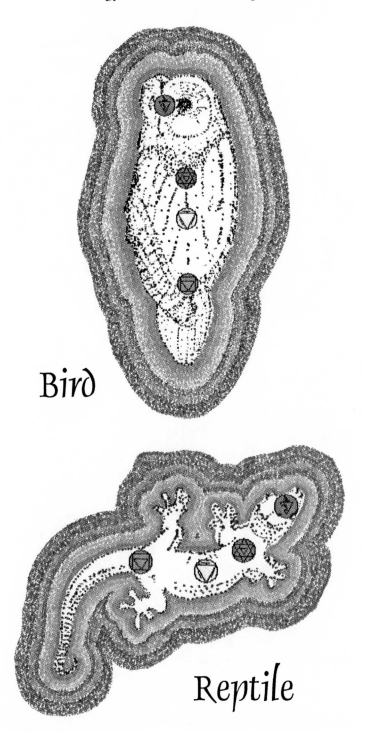

Bird

Reptile

Rodent

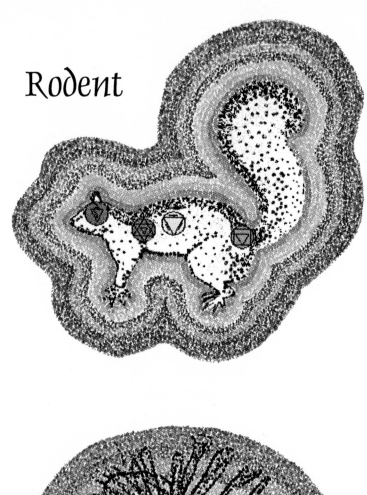

Fish

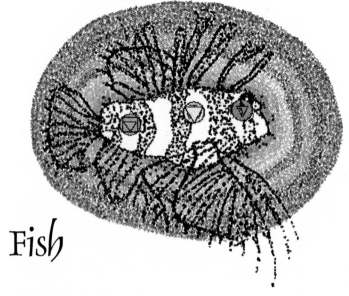

Part Two

Vibrational Remedies

The Doctrine
of Signatures

"The Spirit is the life of the Soul"

Paracelsus was a master physician and philosopher who was born in the late fifteenth century. A true pioneer and rebel in his field, his thought and breakthrough discoveries were unheard of in his time. He acknowledged the essential role of intuition in healing, and that the "universal life force" is responsible for it. He expressed that the Universe and all living things within it exist in an invisible field of light. He saw the spiritual essence behind the forms all around him. He was a practical mystic, and brought his understanding of the nature of Spirit into the world through medicinal plants, spa and mineral therapy, and excellent nutrition. Paracelsus acknowledged wholesome food as a medium for the transmission of life force.

What is known today as the "Doctrine of Signatures" was what the Chinese have used for centuries, and Paracelsus termed the "Doctrine of Sympathetic Resemblances". In this, he stated that all growing things reveal through their structure, form, color, and aroma their peculiar usefulness to human beings. He instructed the physicians of his day to search within themselves for the spiritual insight by which they could recognize and even sense the inherent energies of plants.

Though few of us may be gifted with this kind of innate wisdom and spiritual acumen, there are many mysteries of nature that become easy to decipher when utilizing this simple method of recog-

47

nizing similarities. Paracelsus gave us this important key, a short cut, in discerning the purpose of nature through its very design.

Qualities of Signature

The primary qualities in the design of plant and mineral are color, shape, size, texture, and aroma. By studying these various characteristics, many clues can be given as to the hidden energetic attributes that lie inside. Some signatures in plants are so strong that their qualities are carried through their every form, from the herb, to the essence and even the aroma. This is true for example, with eucalyptus, garlic, and valerian.

Though the hidden clues of signature may at first seem hard to decipher, it takes only an open mind and heart to begin to see with an inner eye what has been before us all along.

Color

All living creatures have energy centers, or chakras, in their bodies. These coordinate and regulate the lifestream of energy throughout the physical body. Each chakra has a corresponding color associated with it (see the Chakra Chart in the Energetic Systems of Animals chapter). With few exceptions, the color of flower or gem corresponds to the chakra of the same color. Also, color is the primary signature for gems and minerals, as shape, odor and texture are not as applicable as in the diversified form of plants. The following pages give several examples of flowers and minerals and their color correspondence with the chakras.

CHAKRA	COLOR	FLOWER	MINERAL
Root chakra	Black		Lava
			Obsidian
			Jet
			Onyx
			Blk. Tourmaline
			Smoky Quartz
			Black Coral
			Black Pearl
			Black Diamond

CHAKRA	COLOR	FLOWER	MINERAL
	Red	Red Spider Lily	Cuprite
		Red Ginger	Bloodstone
		Red Hibiscus	Red Jasper
		Red Poppy	Red Coral
		Red Mtn. Heather	Garnet
		Rosa Gallica	
		Red Amaranthus	
		Scarlet Mimulus	
		Ocotillo Cactus	
		Spice Bush	
		Indian Pink	
		Carob	
Navel Chakra	Orange	Cal. Poppy	Wulfenite
		Marigold	Amber
		Orange Flame	Orange Calcite
		Flower Cactus	Carnelian Agate
		Lion's Tail	
		Monkeyflower Bush	
		Flame Vine	
		Cape Honeysuckle	
Solar Plexus Chakra	Yellow	Sunflower	Citrine Quartz
		Eclipse Rose	Yellow Topaz
		Oregold Rose	Yellow Diamond
		Rosa Hugonis	Yellow Sapphire
		Sourgrass	Yellow Jasper
		Blazing Star	Tiger's Eye
		Mustard	
		Yellow Ladies Slipper	
		Dill	
		Daffodil	
		Witch Hazel	
		St. Johns Wort	
Heart Chakra	Green	Bells of Ireland	Green Calcite
		Sea Lettuce	Green Jasper
		Green Rein Orchid	Amazonite
		Angelica	Chrysoprase
		Papyrus	Aventurine
		Solomon's Seal	
	Pink	Koenign V.	Rose Quartz
		Daenmark	Pink Kunzite
		Betty Prior Rose	Pink Diamond

49

CHAKRA	COLOR	FLOWER	MINERAL
		Rosa Roxburghii	Rhodocrocite
		Shooting Star	Watermelon
		Pink Yarrow	Tourmaline
		Amaryllis	
		Pink Powderpuff	
		Coriander	
Throat Chakra	Blue	Rosemary	Blue Calcite
		Larkspur	Kyanite
		Hopi Blue Corn	Turquoise
		Borage	Aquamarine
		Chicory	Blue Lace Agate
		Starflower	Blue Opal
		Forget-Me-Not	Blue Tourmaline
		Potato	
Brow Chakra	Indigo	Artichoke	Lapis Lazuli
		Hyssop	Blue Sapphire
		Harvest Brodiaea	Azurite
			Sodalite
Crown Chakra	Violet	Blue Flag Iris	Amethyst
		Scarlet Pimpernell	Sugilite
		Violet	Charoite
		Water Violet	Purple Diamond
		Lemon Verbena	
		Judas Tree (Red Bud)	
		Echinacea	
		Eggplant	
		Jacobs Ladder	
		Jicama	
		Hardenbergia	
		Lilac	
		Lavender	
		Pennyroyal	
		Chinese Wisteria	
		Uala	
	White	White Yarrow	White Diamond
		Sweet Alyssum	White Quartz
		Edelweiss	Phenakite
		Lotus	Apophyllite
		Gardenia	Selenite
		Tuberose	Danburite
		Easter Lily	

Shape and Size

The shape of a flower or plant often corresponds to human and animal anatomy. For example, the bleeding heart flower is shaped like a heart, and is a supreme essence for the physical heart, as well as heart-sickness, grief and sorrow. Plants with tall stalks often have a relationship to the spine, and blooms with many "fingers" can show correlation to the nervous system. Large leaved plants, such as hollyhock and burdock, often correspond to the large organs of the body: lungs, liver and skin. Essences from peas and corn lend the ability to thrive in dense, populated areas. Zuchinni and banana have particularly obvious correspondence to fertility and the male sex organ. The very size of the plant and flowers can be revealing. Tall and towering plants, such as sunflower and hollyhock, bring higher spiritual wisdom into the body, and align the chakras through the Central Channel. Miniature roses and tiny blooms provide special assistance to tiny animal species: Shetland ponies, toy and teacup poodles, and pot-bellied pigs for example. Essences gathered from budding flowers are valuable for both babies in utero and infancy. Bell-shaped flowers show qualities of higher self, activating the mind. The walnut looks very much like the brain, in two halves, and energetically affects the neurological tissues. Pomegranate, the fruit of which is many seeded and divided by membranous walls, assists with fertility as well as in supporting the cell wall integrity in the body. Plants that display fuzzy and soft hairs, such as comfrey, correspond to the cilia (hairs) of the lung or intestine. Slimy plants that give sap often soothe respiratory problems, such as coughs and sore throats. Marshmallow and milkweed are two examples.

Even the more esoteric qualities of a flower can often be seen in its shape, as in the mariposa and butterfly lilies. The essence of these flowers provides assistance in shedding of the old-a metamorphosis. This of course is the signature of the butterfly, which the flower resembles. Vibrational remedies assist us in understanding the oneness of creation, and seeing the practical similarities of nature right before our eyes.

The growth rate and cycles of a plant can be a key to its signature. For example, a plant with a rapid growth rate, such as bamboo, provides rapid energy flow into the systems of the body. In some plants the growth rate actually expands and contracts, which has affinity to the blood vessels.

Plants that flower in the beginning of the season can be beneficial for children and adolescents. Conversely, blooms that appear at the end of the year are often keyed to assist the elderly and aging process. And plants with long growing seasons, with flowers that appear early it the year and mature much later, have longevity as their signature, withstanding seasonal and climatic changes. These plants are usually found in the warmer climates, such as date palm.

Flowers that bloom close to the ground provide stabilizing and grounding influence. Vines and climbing plants teach flexibility and encourage growth beyond limitations. Plants with both female and male flowers contain the highest of frequency, balancing female and male energy, as well as left and right hemispheres of the brain.

Texture and Aroma

Plants with rough texture and sharp or pointed leaves are often excellent for treatment of skin problems and lacerations, such as aloe vera and luffa. Both stinging nettle and poison ivy, plants which cause irritation and pain to the body, can soothe inflammation in the body when administered as essences. In the undersea world, pearls are created originally as an irritation in the soft inner lining of the oyster. Essence of pearl is excellent for the treatment of stress and anxiety.

The signature of aroma is much more subtle and challenging to identify. Sometimes the pungency of odor can reveal the potency of the essence, such as with eucalyptus and camphor. And with the potent yet balanced sweetness of jasmine, for example, the remedy can aid hypoglycemia, as well as the ability to smell. As we tune *all* of our senses to the world of nature, we begin to see the hidden gifts that lie just under our noses, before our eyes, and in our hands.

Choosing Essences: Pendulum Dowsing and Kinesiology

Every vibrational remedy has a holographic imprint of energetic support, the whole of which we know little. The research information we have may be accurate, but may also vary greatly with each animal (or person) being treated. The time of day or season of the year an essence is gathered can influence its properties. Lotus essence gathered in India may have similar but unique qualities compared to lotus gathered in Hawaii, for instance. The cycle and process of the animal or person can have affect on the impact of the essence. There is also undoubtedly a myriad array of qualities in each vibrational remedy that has unique influence not necessarily common to all beings. And of course, when the various essences are combined, the healing properties can multiply, fuse and complement each other in ways so individual and specific to each animal or person, that documentation and categorization may never be complete, if indeed possible.

The problem with choosing remedies by their definitions is that the underlying cause is often not addressed. For instance, stress can be caused by anger, frustration, transition, immune system compromise, or chemical exposure, to name but a few factors. It is important to use our deeper sensing, to search below the surface to determine what the core issue is.

Because of the vast repertoire of support present in each and every vibrational remedy, it is safe to say that *each essence has something for everyone*. This means that you **cannot** make a wrong choice. If 99% of an essence's qualities are not necessary for the animal, the remedy for the most part will simply not resonate with her, and will have no affect. The art of proper diagnosing, either through dowsing methods or intuitive guidance, comes with trusting our instincts and what information we receive. Knowing that all remedies are gifts and provide benefit, all we need to do is trust, and let the process work through us, regardless of technique. So, let's have fun with it! Spirit will guide each of us expertly and personally, if we let it.

At times, it can be very beneficial to have working understanding of dowsing and kinesiology techniques. These tools can be efficient ways of getting quick and accurate information, when we need to focus on one or two remedies out of a thousand in a few moments. They can be excellent aides for healing, crisis, and tapping into information hard to access otherwise. However, the importance of these methods of diagnosing and choosing essences is secondary, at best, to our intuition, and should **never** be a substitute for it. It is important to remember that through whatever tool we use, what is being accessed is the animal's inner wisdom. This wisdom is the point, not the tool. As we become more sensitive to this wealth of information by trusting our intuition and the information from our guide teams, the tools become less and less important.

The Pendulum Method

The primary method of dowsing uses a pendulum. Pendulums come in all materials, shapes and sizes. They can be beautifully crafted from gemstones, crystals, woods and metals. They can be as simple as thread tied through a shell or key, and need not be intricate or expensive to work accurately. A pendulum need only feel good in the hand, weighted and well balanced.

It is best to hold the pendulum with at least the thumb and first two fingers of the hand, as the swing will be stronger and more accurate. Be sure the arm is bent and the elbow not resting on any surface. What the pendulum does is tap into the electrical field of the animal that is being tested. As every electrical field has a negative and positive charge, the swing will show either a negative or positive response. (See below.)

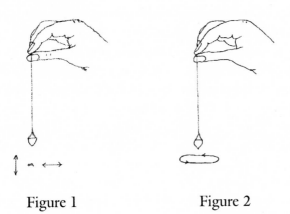

Figure 1   Figure 2

When any method of dowsing is used which taps the electrical system, and involves humans as well as animals when dowsing for them, it will use the water in your bodies. This is because water is the medium for conducting electricity in the body. So, keep water handy for both you and the animal when dowsing.

Also, when asking questions through the pendulum, it is important to remember that you are asking the higher aspect of the animal or her guides, not the pendulum itself. It is a neutral tool, and it's only the indicator. Address the *animal* through the pendulum.

Getting to know the feel of the pendulum can take a little time and practice, or you may get it right away. To begin, ask the pendulum for a positive (yes) swing. This can be a circular motion (clockwise or counter clockwise). Or, it can be a straight line, going up and down or back and forth. Then ask for a negative (no) swing. It may take a while for the pendulum to discernibly move, so be patient. Keep your mind and heart steady on your intent, and wait for the answer. Again, it may take some time to feel and visibly see a response. You can ask for a stronger swing. Once you get the hang of both the yes and no swings, you're ready to go!

It's important to see the pendulum as a diagnostic tool. I never use it as an oracle to get information regarding the future. It doesn't work, anyway. It simply taps into the subconscious and superconscious body of knowledge of what IS. From determining the most nutritious tomato at the grocery store to what mineral your toucan may be missing in his diet, it is about diagnosing what IS. By attempting to use any dowsing technique as an oracle, it will be highly ineffective and inaccurate, at best.

Before I use the pendulum for myself or another, I call in Archangel Michael for his protection three times, so that all information is clear, appropriate, and of the Light of Creation. Tapping into these dimensions can be tricky otherwise.

When dowsing for an animal, first ask if you are able to surrogate for them. If so, proceed. You can specify whether you would like to ask the animal herself, or her guiding support team. It is not necessary to have the animal with you either. It can be thousands of miles away. All questions can be asked that require yes or no answers, and correspond to the positive or negative swings. You can always ask to see what is going on. It's good to stop the pendulum between questions. Sometimes, I'll be following a specific line of questions and the answers will start to get muddy. The pendulums swing will become oblong or chaotic. It may be necessary to drink water or ask different questions or stop altogether. When you are finished, be sure to thank all who have assisted you.

Kinesiology Method

Kinesiology, or muscle checking, is the system of applying gentle pressure to a muscle of the body, which is met by varied degrees of resistance. When a question is posed, and the resisting pressure is weak, it demonstrates that the low energy of the response is a negative answer. Strong resistance would show a strong energetic response, a positive reply which manifests through the muscle reaction. Though more difficult to explain in word and by diagram, these methods are not hard to master, with a little practice and patience. As in pendulum dowsing, kinesiology uses the electrical system of the body, which in turn uses the body's water to conduct the body's electricity. Be sure to be well-hydrated before starting, and have water handy for yourself and the animal that you are surrogating for. As kinesiology requires conscious muscle resistance, it cannot be used directly on an animal—people are necessary to be proxies. However, muscle checking can easily be done on oneself. I find it easiest to use one hand rather than two. One hand may be a bit more difficult to learn, but I have found that it's the best, most efficient and accurate way.

The principle of kinesiology uses *pressure* with one arm, hand or finger, against a *resisting* arm, hand or finger. So, even though you can muscle check using your arm against someone else's arm, or even one hand against your other hand, you can most easily use one finger against another finger of the same hand. The resistance may be subtler this way, but is very streamlined.

Using the first finger (pointing finger) as the muscle indicator (or resisting muscle), hold it straight and taut. You may use either your right or left hand. Using the middle finger right next to it to apply pressure, bend it until the pad of the first joint of the finger is pressing just below the nail of the pointing finger. Press against finger A with finger B and deliberately resist the pressure. This is a strong, positive response. See **Figure 3** below:

Figure 3

Now, press again and deliberately relax the pointing finger of any resistance. You will feel the hand go weak and close into a soft fist. See **Figure 4** below:

Figure 4

Practice both ways several times until you can easily feel the difference. A circuit of positive electrical energy runs throughout the body at all times. Holding the fingers as in the above diagram, represents this actual circuit. When a question is posed that has positive response, the circuit remains positive. The pointing finger will remain taut. When the response is no, it breaks the positive circuit and becomes negative (see **Fig. 4** above). The hand will then collapse into a soft fist. Begin by asking questions with answers you know-such as your name, gender, etc. Then ask questions with sure no answers. This will start the process for you of understanding the two responses. When comfortable with the process, ask if you may surrogate for the animal in her behalf, and if the time is appropriate. If it's a go, I proceed.

The day on Earth is coming when assistance of this nature will no longer be necessary, and our intuition, which is our individual voice of Spirit, will be sufficient. Until that time, we can be thankful for and proficient at utilizing these methods of support and access to the healing process.

Essence Usage
and Administration

The complex and sometimes neurotic psychological make-up of the human psyche can be somewhat of a challenge for vibrational remedies to work through. With animals, the purity and simplicity of their consciousness and psyche allow the essences to have immediate impact and potent effect. It is often advisable for those who are treating their own animals, or for practitioners who are doing in-house treatment, to ingest the essence along with the animal. This allows for full effect, and will also be sure to address the same issues that may be present in the people involved.

Administering vibrational remedies to animals should be simple and non-invasive. It is important to remember that essences are vibrational and therefore do not need to run through the physical body to work. Often the administration of traditional allopathic medicines can be uncomfortable and even painful. With essences, it should be an enjoyable experience for everyone concerned.

When approaching an animal to give them essences, I always do so with an attitude of respect and assistance. It is important to explain what's coming, and after they have experienced these remedies, they will indeed understand what they are and will look forward to taking them. It is easy for them to sense the life energy they carry. And, when the essence is no longer needed, the animal will often lose interest in taking it.

Try not to touch the mouth or any part of the animal's body with the dropper, as bacteria will get on the dropper and into the bottle. A good rule of thumb is to not touch the dropper to *anything*. And, be sure to place the correct dropper into the correct bottle, as their properties will become corrupted if mixed.

Starlight elixirs are the most delicate of vibrational remedies. The bottles should never be opened in direct sunlight. When I am using them inside, I only open the star bottles in dim light or candlelight. When outside, I open the bottles for brief periods of time under cover or in the shade.

When placing essences into water bowls or troughs for livestock, the drops can be stirred in the water for several seconds to activate the essences. The bottle should always be shaken vigorously for several seconds before used, again, to activate the essences. Administration via water and food is the easiest way, however, many animals (especially cats) can be extremely sensitive to *any* strange substance in their food or water, especially alcohol, so I recommend rubbing essences lightly into the ear tips, paws or into the gums (if the animal likes that). Simply place a few drops on your fingers, and rub them in. My puppy loves to lap it up from the palm of my hand.

For birds, they love showers, so the best way they like to receive remedies is from lukewarm water in a spray bottle. Also, alcohol is not good for a bird's system, and it's best not to put essences in their drinking water. Birds that enjoy being handled love to have essences gently rubbed into their necks.

As vibrational remedies don't have to run through the physical body to affect the energetic bodies, rubbing essences on the external body can be very effective if your animal doesn't mind. Rubbing a few drops into chakra points, over various organs or the top of the head works very well.

For the exact dosage for your animal, I recommend either pendulum dowsing or muscle checking (see the Choosing Essences chapter). However, a basic dosage is 2-3 drops 2-3 times daily for most animals, or a full dropperful in the food or water bowl *daily*, for larger animals. With vibrational remedies, it isn't the quantity, but how often it is given. Animals need much less than people, and usually the duration is much shorter.

After essence bottles are opened, they can lose some of their potency. Placing bottles under a pyramid (six inches apart under large pyramids) for two hours will restore them to original potency. See Resource Chapter for pyramids.

An excellent way to thoroughly cleanse and permeate the house with essences is when cleaning. A few drops in the mop water can leave the floor especially sparkling. Just a bit added to natural cleaning supplies, from bathroom cleanser to window wash solution to carpet shampoo, can really make a difference in a home for all who live there. When moving into a new house, a few drops of cedar or pennyroyal essence in soapy water can pull out negative or dead energy when used to clean the walls, floors, cabinets, etc. Often, this can settle an animal right down in new circumstances, when they may be sensitive to the energy of the previous tenants.

With the administration of *all* vibrational remedies, it is helpful and more effective to call in the assistance of nature, and her helping, guiding spirits. The devas of the individual flowers and gems, the overlighting Beings of the planets, stars and suns, and the elemental overseers of sacred sites and environmental places of power are all available to help us. We can never have too much assistance! And they are here especially to aid us in the healing of our animal friends.

Healing Crisis

Occasionally, when using energetic remedies and healing modalities, animals may experience what is called a "healing crisis". Though it may not happen often, it's good to be aware of its symptoms when it does occur. The healing crisis is simply an intensification or worsening of the problematic condition, as part of the healing process. It is usually not severe and rarely lasts more than several days.

Though the healing crisis is more unusual with energetic modalities, it can occur because it is the body's way of eliminating toxins. The healing crisis is a natural life process of cleansing and regeneration. If essences are being given for fear or anger, for instance, the animal may display more fearful or angry behavior, or show physical symptoms such as rash, cough, fatigue or diarrhea. Also, if a deep-seated physical condition has been present in the body for a long time and vibrational medicines begin to bring it to the surface to heal and clear, the symptoms may be uncomfortable and even severe. During this time, plenty of rest, water and calm should be offered. Animals need as much quiet as is possible in the home, and only loving affection if they welcome it. Aromatherapy and soothing music are often beneficial. Additional essences may be necessary. After a healing crisis occurs, animals are usually back to their old selves in a few days, and often feel better than ever. An energy boost is not uncommon.

So, with any therapy, if your animal should show symptoms of a healing crisis, know it is short-lived and nature's process of healing.

The Five Chinese Elements and Essence Correlation

Vibrational remedies carry within them the essential elements and forces of nature. The climate and environment where they grow or blossom are the keys to the element they represent. When these are correlated to the five elements of traditional Chinese medicine: metal, fire, wood, earth and water, their healing qualities can be better understood. For example, the lotus is a water lily, and of the water element. The water element in Chinese medicine corresponds to the kidneys, bladder and filtering of toxins. Therefore, lotus essence can aid these organs and the body in the process of cleansing. When certain organs or body systems are weak or out of balance, essences from the needed element can be very beneficial. If the animal is experiencing fiery anger or frustration, for instance, an essence or two from the water element can be very balancing.

As flowers that grow in the water carry the water force in the essence, such as water lilies, pond and marsh plants, seaweeds and lunar (night) blooming plants, the fire element is most often re-vealed in desert solar (day) blooming flowers, such as aloe vera and saguaro cactus. The wood element can be found in flowering tree and woodland essences, including apple, aspen and lemon, as well as some ferns, mosses and lichens. Essences that carry the earth force are numerous and varied. Those that grow close to the ground, often in the mountains, or have the deepest and most complex root systems are of the Earth element. The metal element is carried in the essences made from metals themselves, such as gold, silver, and copper.

According to ancient Chinese medicine, the element of water governs the kidneys, urinary bladder, immune system, teeth, ears and bones, and corresponds to the emotion of fear. The fire element governs the heart, pericardium and small intestines and circulation as well as the emotion of joy. Wood governs the liver, gall bladder, blood and tendons and carries the emotion of anger. The earth element corresponds to the spleen, pancreas, stomach and digestion, and relates to worry. The metal element governs the lungs and respiration, as well as the emotions of grief and sadness. The following charts and diagram further illustrate the elements and corresponding essences.

FIVE ELEMENTS CHARTS AND QUALITIES

METAL		
BODY SYSTEMS	PHYSICAL INDICATIONS	EMOTIONAL INDICATIONS
Lungs Respiration Excretion Mucous	Asthma Bronchitis Allergy Coughing Wheezing Shallow Breathing Phlegm	Grief Sadness

FIRE		
BODY SYSTEMS	PHYSICAL INDICATIONS	EMOTIONAL INDICATIONS

Heart
Pericardium
  (Heart Protector)
Circulation
Emotional Response
Mental Response
Digestion
Vital Functions
	Heart Malfunction
	Heart Disease
	Mental Changes &
	  Trauma
	Behav. Changes &
	  Trauma
	Nervous Urination
	Insecurity
	Constipation
	Fatigue
	Weight Loss
	Thirst
		Joy
		Happiness
		Emo. Changes &
		  Trauma

The Five Chinese Elements and Essence Correlation

WOOD		
BODY SYSTEMS	PHYSICAL INDICATIONS	EMOTIONAL INDICATIONS
Liver	Blood Disorders	Anger
Gall Bladder	Constipation	Aggression
Blood	Infertility	Frustration
Central Nervous System	Dizziness	Resentment
Skin	Brittle Nails & Fur	Hostility
Intestines	Fatigue	Depression
Joints	Spaying & Neutering	Stubborn Behavior
Tendons	Eye Problems	
Eyes	Seizures	
Moisturizing of Sex Organs	Excessive Barking	
	Hepatitis	

EARTH		
BODY SYSTEMS	PHYSICAL INDICATIONS	EMOTIONAL INDICATIONS
Spleen	Weight Loss	Worry
Pancreas	Vomiting	Apathy
Stomach	Diarrhea	Lethargy
Digestion	Exhaustion	
Muscle Tone	Burping	
	Abdominal Discomfort	
	Soft Stools	
	Loss or Increase of Appetite	
	Poor Digestion	
	Gas	
	Constipation	
	Fatigue	
	Bad Breath	
	Diabetes	
	Eating strange things	
	Motion Sickness	
	Poor Muscle Tone	

WATER		
BODY SYSTEMS	PHYSICAL INDICATIONS	EMOTIONAL INDICATIONS
Kidneys	Renal Failure	Fear
Urinary Bladder	Cystitis	Emotional
Bones	Runt of Litter	Oversensitivity
(Marrow & Cortex)	Joint Stiffness	Timidity
Teeth	Hip Dysplasia &	Withdrawal
Carries Water &	Malformed Bones	
Nutrients into	Arthritis	
Body	Dental Problems	
Filters Toxins Out	Osteoporosis	
Hydration	Dehydration	
Immune System	Swelling	
Ears	Colds	
Sweat Glands	Bladder Infection	
Feces	Ear Problems	
Urine	Itching & Scratching	
Saliva	Dryness of Organs, Scalp, Skin and Paws	
Hormones	Overheating	
	Thirst	
	Dry Mouth	
	Constipation	
	Vomiting of Food	
	Dry Cough	
	Small, Rapid Pulse	
	Cold Intolerance	
	Frequent Urination	
	Hormonal Imbalance	
	Incontinence	
	Disc Problems	
	Gurgling Belly	

Listed below are several examples of essences which carry the energy of the five individual Chinese elements. This list is by no means complete, but will give you a solid foundation.

THE FIVE ELEMENTS AND CORRESPONDING ESSENCES

Metal	Fire	Wood
Brass	Agave	Almond
Bronze	Agave Yaquiana	Apple
Carbon Steel	Aloe Vera	Apricot
Chromium	Candy Barrel Cactus	Aspen
Copper	Compass Barrel Cactus	Avocado
Gallium	Desert Barrel Cactus	Balsam Poplar
Gold	Flame of the Forest	Date Palm
Magnesium	Hedgehog Cactus	Beech
Manganese	Jumping Cholla Cactus	Black Spruce
Molybdenum	Klein Pencil Cholla Cactus	Bo Tree
Palladium	Lobivia Cactus	Cedar
Platinum	Pegasus Orchid Cactus	Cherry
Silver	Milky Nipple Cactus	Chestnut Bud
Tin	Prickly Pear Cactus	Cinnamon
Zinc	Noble Star Flower Cactus	Elm
	Ocotillo	Eucalyptus
	Queen of the Night	Grapefruit
	Saguaro	Hawthorne
	Staghorn Cholla Cactus	Kamani
	Teddy Bear Cholla Cactus	Kiwi
	Waikiki Rainbow Cactus	Locust
	Woven Spine Pineapple Cactus	Loquat
	Yucca	Macadamia
		Magnolia
		Maple
		Nectarine
		Oak
		Olive
		Orange
		Pear
		Peach
		Pine
		Redwood
		Spruce
		Walnut

Water
Bamboo
Bog Blueberry
Cat's Tail
Evening Primrose
Green Bog Orchid
Irish Moss
Kelp
Lotus
Rice
Scotch Moss
Sea Lettuce
Shooting Star
Swamp Onion
Water Violet

Earth
Carrot
Chives
Dandelion
Garlic
Horseradish
Kohlrabi
Onion
Potato
Radish
Red Mountain Heather
Squash (all varieties)
Strawberry

Vibrational Remedies— The Heart of Nature

"Essences provide the opportunity to commune directly with nature."

The next several chapters address the various types of vibrational remedies: flower, gem, starlight, environmental, sacred site and element. The individual descriptions are based on information that has been gathered up until now, through case histories, documented data from essence developers and practitioners, as well as channeled sources. Please use them as guidelines only. If you feel drawn to any particular gem or star, for instance, or your animal will **not** keep his nose out of a certain blossom, use it. It is most assuredly the right one. Instincts are to be trusted, especially in the world of energy. Besides, it is impossible to pick a wrong essence. There is something in every vibrational remedy for everyone!

Flower Essences

"...(Flower essences) are able, like beautiful music or any glorious or
uplifting thing which gives us inspiration, to raise our very natures.
They provide creative patterns of harmony that bring us nearer
to our souls and by that very act bring us peace and relieve suffering.
They cure by flooding the body with the beautiful vibrations
of the Highest nature ... in whose presence, there is the opportunity
for disease to melt away like snow in the sunshine."
—Dr. Edward Bach

Flower essences share a unique relationship with the animals of
this world. Animals are precious and dearly loved by nature and the
devic realm. Flower essences provide the opportunity to commune
directly with nature. The delicate emotional, mental and even spiritual aspects of animals can be greatly enhanced and supported with
vibrational remedies made from flowers.

The highest consciousness and finest qualities of all plants and
trees manifest in the flower. To capture this conscious energy in
vibrational remedies, peak blossoms are placed in a bowl of pure
water and solar infused in morning sunlight or moonlight. This is
the process of energetic transference. What is carried and imprinted
into the water is the energetic blueprint of the flower, unified with
and activated by the power of the sun or moon. The powerful union
of solar or lunar and flower energies in water becomes the mother
tincture. This mother tincture is blended in equal parts with alcohol
(usually brandy), vinegar or shiso to preserve it. Final dilution into
stock and dosage strength is less than one part per several hundred.
When making any mother tincture, a genuine attitude of reverence
and emptiness allows the purest, highest energy to be transferred

into the water. Any negative thought-forms or emotions will negatively impact the essence, and have just the opposite effect of healing!

Exactly how this process of energetic transference works is not completely understood. Indigenous peoples have made essences from flowers for centuries. Channeled information from various sources cite both Lemuria and Atlantis as cultures that utilized the energy of flowers extensively. Many healers and highly sensitive people have understood the underlying signature of flowers. Paracelsus, Hildegard of Bingen, Rudolph Steiner, George Washington Carver and Luther Burbank are a few. In the 1920s, Dr. Edward Bach began to discover the healing qualities of flower essences. Dr. Bach was a physician (pathologist and bacteriologist), an intuitive, and healer. Flowers conveyed to him directly, through touch or taste, their specific healing qualities. He developed thirty-eight flower essences, many made from trees, and are still widely in use today.

Flower essences are now being made by companies and individuals all over the world. Each region and climate has its own dynamic and character that comes through the vibrational remedies. Many essences gathered in Alaska, for example, carry the rugged male energy of the mountain wilderness. Cactus flowers captured in the desert are very feminine and distinctly individual. (Have you ever heard of a meadow of cacti?) Coastal wildflowers carry the powerful feminine energy of the ocean, and essences made from flowers in remote wilderness are strongly devic in signature. Flower essence manufacturers are now producing in the Dutch Alps, Australia and the Australian Bush, England, Russia, many European countries, Canada, Alaska, the Southwest desert, the Rocky Mountains, Sierra Nevada, the Blue Ridge Mountains, the Cascades and Coastal Mountains. As time progresses, we will see flower essences being made in every country, by companies and individuals. There are myriad gifts that flowers of the world are waiting to share, and the days are coming when they will be readily available to all.

Flower Essence Qualities

*"All flowers talk to me and so do hundreds of little living things
in the woods. I learn what I know by watching and loving everything."*
—George Washington Carver

Acacia- Good for group harmony. Cleanses the energy system.

Aconite- For deep inner calm. Energy balancer.

Agave- Excellent for trauma and abuse recovery. For fear and lack of trust. Provides comfort and empowerment.

Agrimony- Use when bleeding, especially when accompanied by anxious behavior. Good for restlessness.

Allamanda- Effective for post-op recovery, and frailty. Provides inner strength and confidence. A convalescing essence. Provides balance and strength during transition. Aids hearing problems.

Almond- Excellent birth essence. Promotes mother-infant bonding.

Aloe Ciliaris- Reputed to reduce cancerous cell growth.

Aloe Eru- Soothing and healing after psychic bombardment. Assists recuperation from lengthy kennel and vet visits.

Aloe Vera- Eases all healing crises. Excellent for healing of tissues and digestive tract.

Alpine Pussy Paws- For the animal who wanders. Helps to keep the focus on home.

Alpine Azalea- Indicated for animals who are indoors and/or disconnected from nature. Provides attunement with the angelic realm. Heals and releases heart wounds, especially from neglect.

Alyssum- Carries the support and nurturance of Mother God. Eases extreme behaviors. Strengthening, balancing, harmonizing. Empowers female aspects and soothes aggressive male behavior. Excellent for mothers and their young.

Amaranthus- Provides support and courage during tragedy and loss. Lifts grief. Balancing. Aligns all bodies. Good epilepsy remedy. Grounding and stabilizing, especially for animals that are withdrawn and disassociated. Helps animals to realign with the departed.

Andalisa- Protects and supports the immune system.

Angelica- Provides spiritual and angelic support. Knits wounds and injuries on all levels.

Angel's Trumpet- For assisting animals to surrender into death without fear.

Apple- Promotes health, warmth and comfort. Cleansing and nurturing. Releases fear. Assists the ability to flow with life.

Apricot- General tonic and strengthener for animals. Excellent for canine and feline cancers, leukemia, HIV.

Arnica- Primary essence for recovery of abuse, injury, sickness, shock and trauma. Aids in body/soul fusion.

Artichoke- Helps release grief and sadness.

Asparagus- Assists animals who are subjected to and sensitive to negative human thought-forms and energy. Provides psychic protection.

Aspen- Helps to move animal through extreme fear, mistrust, nervousness, anxiety and timidity. Provides comfort in new or unfamiliar circumstances. Excellent remedy for wild animals.

Avocado- Assists in intimacy and bonding issues. Allays the fear of being touched. Eases mistrust and withdrawal. Promotes memory. Good training essence. Aids the function of all eliminative organs and digestion. Helps to release suppressed emotions.

Baby Blue Eyes- Indicated for poor boundary issues. Provides self-esteem.

Balm of Gilead- Eases the birth experience. Indicated for poor maternal instincts.

Balsam Poplar- Excellent for indoor animals. Synchronizes internal body rhythms with planetary rhythms. Good remedy for trauma and abuse, releasing sexual tension. Indicated for stud animals.

Bamboo- Alleviates stress by opening the flow of energy to the energy system. Aligns chakras.

Bamboo Orchid- Improves self-esteem issues from neglect, trauma or abuse. Restores faith and trust in the animal for himself and others.

Banana- Excellent for issues involving teeth, gums and facial bones, as well as spinal difficulties, particularly sacral.

Banksia Baxtena- For balance of male sexual energy. Excellent for wild animals, studs, horses. Opens the lower chakras.

Barley- Indicated for anger, aggression and instability. Excellent for horses who have experienced trauma. Cleanses and balances the energy system. Very grounding.

Basil- For anxiety, bickering and hysteria. Promotes group harmony. Alleviates emotional and mental fatigue. Indicated for depression.

Bear Grass- For animals with attitude. Attunes animals to humans and each other. Assists learning and training modalities. Restores balance.

Beech- Eases intolerance for other animals or people. Remedies emotional isolation. Promotes group harmony. Provides gentle expansiveness and guidance. Good for the oversensitive animal. Indicated for allergies and all skin hypersensitivity.

Bells of Ireland- Especially for outdoor animals. Enhances vocal communication with nature, and helps to connect with angels and nature. Assists all blockages. Aids in tissue regeneration.

Bignonia- For lethargy and lack-luster approach to life. Increases the life force.

Birch- Aids recovery from abuse and hurtful relationship. Dissolves fears of rejection. Fosters trust and acceptance.

Bistort- Aids disorientation. Very strengthening and grounding.

Bittersweet- For grief, mourning and despondency. Uplifts, heals and soothes.

Blackberry- Aids neurotic behaviors common in captive animals. Relieves depression. Good for wild animals, animals in zoos, sanctuaries, etc. Also indicated for elderly animals. Restores the hope and joy of life. Aids kidneys, liver, heart and lungs. Stimulates endocrine system. For respiratory ailments. Helps in absorption of vitamins and minerals.

Black Currant- Excellent for healing trauma deep in the cellular memory of all species. Brings health and vitality.

Black-Eyed Susan- First-aid shock essence. Excellent for stress. Aids low self-esteem. Provides joy and brightness as well as emotional stability. Energy system strengthener. Opens heart to unconditional love of oneself and all creation.

Black Spruce- Aids learning difficulties, seemingly uncontrollable "bad behavior", cat spraying, and improper elimination.

Blazing Star- Opens the heart to expressing love and connecting to God.

Bleeding Heart- Assists in letting go during panic, grief and loss of a loved one. Eases relationship dependency issues. Provides peaceful loving energy and trust. Helps to release painful emotional attachments. Enhances soothing effect of music.

Bloodroot- Purifies the blood, as well as all other levels of being. Allows release of old judgements, bringing inner peace. Excellent for cats and horses.

Bo Tree- Helps attune animals to higher psychic energy. Lifts cellular memory and trauma from past lifetimes of abuse. Excellent for wild birds in temporary captivity.

Bog Blueberry- Remedies stagnation, malaise, lethargy and depression. Indicated for resistance to life.

Bog Rosemary- Helps animals release fear of other animals. Promotes trust.

Borage- Powerful heart healer on all levels. Provides courageous support during the grief and letting go process. Provides upliftment for depression, illness and aging.

Bottlebrush- Use sparingly. For treatment of trauma and stress from kennels, the pound, breeders, aquarium fish and aviaries.

Bougainvillea- Excellent for soul loss. Inspirational and emotionally fulfilling, helps animals to reconnect to the magical aspects of life.

Buffalo Gourd- Indicated for exhaustion, emotional imbalance, nervous
system depletion, vulnerability and over-sensitivity. Provides balance,
confidence and stability.

Butterfly Lily-Provides encouragement, upliftment and strength. Relieves
stress. Good training essence.

Cacao- Excellent for relieving stress. Amplifies homeopathic remedies.

Calendula- Helps to release fear. Provides psychic protection against
negative energy and thought-forms. Provides alignment with Inner
Light, and connection to healing energies of the Earth. Strengthens
connection to other species, nature and the devic realms.

California Bay Laurel- Indicated for nervous system imbalances. Relieving
and soothing.

California Buckeye- Improves self-esteem. Especially for indoor animals.
Enhances attunement with nature and nature spirits.

California Pitcher Plant- Primary essence for releasing animals into the
wild. Provides connection to Spirit and balanced grounding in new
environment. Grounding for animals in shock that are disassociated
with the world around them.

California Poppy- Indicated for animals with behavior problems. Lends
emotional balance and support in releasing negative and destructive
emotions.

California Wild Rose- As with all roses, provides supreme heart healing and
support, especially after trauma. Opens the heart to love and trust.
Useful in treating lick granuloma.

Calla Lily- Opens the heart to experience and express love. Provides insight
and understanding of the human realm.

Calliandra- A profound heart healer. Clears emotional blockages. Promotes fur growth.

Calothamnus Validus- For animals living in environments that carry negative thought-forms. Strengthens boundaries. Provides psychic protection.

Candlenut Tree- Good essence for group harmony. Deeply calming and
opening. Provides ease in relating to and understanding others.

Candy Barrel Cactus- Assists self-esteem issues, eases deep agitation and
lack of focus. Provides calm, focus and peace.

Cantaloupe- Uplifting and calming. Brings the joy of living.

Canyon Grapevine (Wild Grapevine)- Indicated for co-dependency, lack of
boundaries and taking on of human toxicity. Provides psychic protection. For animals that are withdrawn and alienated. Excellent for group
harmony.

Cape Honeysuckle- Excellent for grief, loneliness and difficult emotional
states. Provides balance.

Carob- Provides assistance in attuning to higher psychic energies. Excellent for all animals in new situations, especially fish and horses.

Cassandra- Especially for indoor animals. Establishes the bond of communication with nature.

Catnip- Indicated for indoor animals, especially cats. Releases stress and irrational fears.

Cat's Tail- Good for group harmony, and emotional balance in large groups. Good for transition.

Cayenne- Provides catalyst for change and aids in releasing stuck patterns of behavior. Good for learning and training difficulties.

Cedar- Supreme cleansing essence for all levels of the body. Indicated for allergies, immune system compromise, and skin problems. Empowering. Provides inner strength. Strengthens boundaries. Lends courage and perseverance to move through anger, fear and self-doubt.

Centaury- Indicated for weakness and tiredness. Immune system booster and re-energizer.

Cerato- Indicated for wild animals temporarily held in captivity. Good for aging animals.

Chamomile- Excellent stress remedy. Excellent for emotional upset manifesting in vomiting and upset stomach. Alleviates barking. Aids wild animals that must be in captivity. Provides attunement to nature. Calming and centering.

Chaparral- Excellent remedy for loneliness, alienation, sadness and withdrawal. Restores connection to Source. Frees nervous tension held in body.

Chaulmoogra Hydnocarpus- Useful in treating animals that are holding human diseases in their body, such as cancer, HIV, leukemia. Provides psychic protection and supports healthy boundaries.

Cherry- Promotes cheerfulness.

Cherry Plum- Relieves extreme tension and stress. For animals who have surrendered to fear. For pain and itching.

Chervil- Excellent essence for the newborn of any species.

Chestnut Bud- Promotes positive learning experience in training, releasing of old patterns of behavior and positive adjustment to new. To aid recovery of a chronic condition. For slow development.

Chicory- Indicated particularly for young animals that are territorial, clingy, jealous and possessive, demanding inappropriate attention. Provides warmth of unconditional love. Excellent for constipation.

Chiming Bells- Especially for indoor animals. Increases awareness of the angelic realm in nature. Excellent for regeneration and renewal. Lifts depression to joy.

Choke Cherry- Aids difficult relationships. Brings clarity and peace.

Chrysanthemum- Indicated for depression and anxiety. Brings emotional calm.

76

Cinnamon- Indicated for heart trauma. Provides emotional calm. Heart balancer.

Clarkia- Excellent for forgiveness, especially when ill emotions are held in the DNA from centuries of abuse and trauma.

Clematis- Provides resilience, calm and inner strength during challenge and crisis. Good for heat related trauma and injury (fire, sunstroke, itching, fever) and shock. Calms emotional tensions. Grounding. Restores peace and balance.

Clove Tree- Excellent for stress, hypertension and anxiety. Brings emotional calm.

Coconut- Provides nourishing upliftment. Brings in the loving support of Mother God. Good birthing essence. Spine, nervous system and energy system strengthener.

Coffee- Helps animals to commune with humans, especially aquatic creatures. Good training essence.

Cohosh (Black)- Aids in the release of cellular tension and lodged thought-forms. Releases blocks. Regenerates relationships.

Columbine- Excellent remedy for abuse and neglect. Restores sense of beauty and self-esteem. Promotes sweetness.

Comandra- For indoor animals. Restores a deep connection with the plant realm and nature in general.

Comfrey- Primary remedy for spay and neuter surgery recovery. Good first-aid remedy after trauma. For disassociation from the body. Assists in healing of nerve damage, and wounds in the energy field. Cleanses, strengthens and restores the nervous system. Telepathic aid.

Compass Barrel Cactus- For anger and grumpiness. Provides lightness and clarity, peace and trust.

Coral Root- Excellent remedy for abuse history. Releases trauma from deep levels and initiates healing.

Coral Root (Spotted)- Rids body of antibiotics and drugs from surgical procedures.

Corn- Especially for crowded indoor and city animals with little access to nature. Also remedies disassociation from body due to illness or trauma. Restores mental vitality.

Cosmos- Excellent essence for telepathy between animals and humans, especially aquatic animals. Good training essence, particularly for show animals. Allays stubbornness and hyper behavior. Excellent healing remedy for horses, and facilitates high communication with humans when hearts are open. Aids in verbal communication and understanding. Helps to achieve pregnancy.

Cotton- Etherically cleansing. Strengthening to the nervous system. Excellent remedy for fear and stress as well as post-op recovery.

Cotton Grass- Excellent for shock, trauma and surgery recovery. Restores balance to the body. Nurturing. Good topical remedy for external trauma.

Cottonwood- Excellent for shock and trauma. Grounding. Promotes the enjoyment and comfort of the physical body.

Cow Parsnip- Provides peace and contentment during times of transition. Helps animals to adapt to new surroundings more quickly. Relieves overwhelm, over-sensitivity and disconnection from life. Welcomes play, fun and happiness.

Coyote Mint- Excellent essence for dogs who have lost their "wild spark". Both grounding and uplifting. A very good remedy for depression in all animals.

Crab Apple- Especially indicated for despondency. A good learning and training essence, assists in breaking bad habits. Aids in cleansing of all bodies. For oversensitivity, allergies, mites and parasites, tooth plaque. For cleansing after poisoning and toxicity. Alleviates runny nose and sneezing. Good for dull or oily fur. Eases inflammation. Good for diarrhea.

Crocus (White)- Good transition essence. Provides support during new cycles, new homes and new beginnings. Excellent birth essence for mother and infant.

Cucumber- Indicated for despair and depression.

Curry Leaf Tree- Promotes group harmony, especially between animals and humans. Fosters relaxed playfulness.

Daffodil- Enhances telepathy and attunement to other animals. Attunes all beings to the source of God within.

Daisy- Aids in animal communication.

Dahlia- Indicated for extreme emotional stress. Alleviates all stress. Integrates emotions. Stimulates faith, confidence and stamina.

Dandelion- Excellent remedy for epilepsy. Releases trauma, tension and stress from physical body, particularly in musculature as well as energy system. Relieves stress from travel. Restores resilience to body. Provides emotional calm. Grounding. Excellent remedy for both wild and domestic birds.

Date Palm- Promotes sweetness and tenderness. Rejuvenating. Encourages life force energy into the cells.

Delphinium- Excellent for indoor animals, as it attunes them to nature, nature spirits and higher purpose.

Desert Barrel Cactus- Promotes clear, strong boundaries and proper relationship.

Devil's Club- Excellent for indoor animals. Promotes deep connection with the Earth and physical body. Provides nourishment and support.

Dill- For stress and overload of all systems. Good for transition and travel needs.

Dog Rose- Indicated for apathy and lethargy. Increases vitality and interest in life.

Dogwood- Excellent remedy for indoor animals. Increases appreciation and attunement to nature. Transcends jealousy and fosters appreciation and communication with others in the environment. Increases aesthetic appreciation. Provides loving inclusiveness.

Dracaena- A nurturing essence that opens the heart to the love of Mother God. Good for birthing issues. Indicated for trauma and abuse history.

Dutchman's Breeches- Primary essence for clearing emotional residue from the aura and the environment. Provides psychic protection, especially for sensitive animals.

Dwarf Fireweed- Excellent trauma remedy. Cleanses all bodies. Transforms unresolved painful and traumatic issues to joy.

Easter Lily- Excellent remedy for epilepsy. Recommended for trauma and post-surgery, especially spay and neutering procedures.

Echinacea- Eases all difficulty with change and transition.

Edelweiss- Provides access to instinctual nature. Good for wild animals that must be in captivity.

Eggplant- Dispels negativity in all bodies. Helps to dissolve cysts and tumors. Give internally and on external tumor.

Elecampagne- Indicated for extreme stress. Provides ease and balance.

Elephant's Head- Provides primary support from the angelic realm. Strengthens ability to perceive and work with Earth energy. Good for indoor animals.

Elm- Aids domestic animals in shedding stress and overwhelm during intense family cycles. Restores compassion and self-value, confidence and upliftment. Alleviates nosebleeds from injury. Indicated for the sudden onset of disease. Aids constipation.

Endive- Indicated for animals in healing crisis or who are having difficulty healing.

Ephedra- Good for trauma and abuse, lack of focus, and loss of will and soul. Provides healing and calm. Fosters confidence, faith and trust.

Eucalyptus- Brings joy and well being. Opens and deepens breathing and movement with life flow.

Evening Primrose- Excellent abuse and neglect remedy, especially regarding mother wounds. A night-blooming (lunar) flower, it provides feminine support. Healing and supportive of new bonding and trust, both mother-infant and animal to human. Good spay and neuter recovery remedy.

Evening Star- Excellent for self-esteem issues related to abuse or neglect. Indicated for aloofness, withdrawal and disconnectedness. Especially for cats. Restores intimacy in relationships, fosters self-esteem.

Fairy Duster- For all nervous system imbalance and hypersensitivity. Grounding, balancing and aligning. Very soothing.

Fennel- Excellent for grief and depression. Alleviates stress caused by humans in the environment. Uplifting. Provides strength and balance.

Feverfew- Works at the deepest cellular level to dispel fear, anger, and despair. Excellent for horses, and all animals who have suffered trauma.

Fig- Eases fear and conflict. Improves confidence.

Figwort- Excellent for agitation, anxiety, fear and poor disposition. Eases emotional stress.

Fireweed- Supreme trauma and shock remedy. Releases trauma from all levels of being. Removes anger. Cleanses energy patterns from body, regenerates etheric, emotional and physical body. Grounding and reconnecting. Excellent for body/soul fusion.

Flame of the Forest- Accelerates purification and physical cleansing. Excellent for stuck and anti-social behaviors. Enhances group harmony.

Forget-Me-Not- Excellent spay and neuter remedy. Alleviates loneliness as well as accidents. Brings in joy, innocence and integration. Assists learning and training. Helps animals face death and transition.

Foxglove- Eases depression and broken heart from loss. Promotes peacefulness. Good remedy for the feet. Releases muscle tension and chaos from the physical heart. Provides connection to devic realm. Uplifting and enlightening. Provides stamina. Good for birds and wild animals. Good for travel.

Frangipani- Indicated for shyness and nervousness. Healing to the throat chakra.

French Marigold- Good for treatment of shock and withdrawal. Promotes openhearted trust. Especially for wild captive animals, birds in particular. For all hearing disorders. Good anti-viral.

Freesia- Excellent remedy for cage stress and stays in kennels or carriers. Cleanses the energy system.

Fuschia- Relieves neuroses, fear and aggression. Opens heart and promotes sweetness. Excellent for the young.

Gardenia- Opens the connection to nature. Lifts depression. Good for indoor animals.

Garlic- Releases fear and anger. Good for nervousness and fright. Cleansing of all bodies of parasites of all kinds.

Gentian- Good for deep interspecies communication. Relieves extensive plaque growth. Aids poor digestion. Indicated for self-doubt, discouragement, and emotional apathy.

Geranium- Gives the ability to awaken understanding of past relationships and to balance and heal them.

Gilia (Scarlet)- Excellent for indoor birds, in increasing their attunement to plants and nature.

Ginger- Promotes deep, cellular relaxation. Energizing and stimulating to the nervous system. Enhances aromatherapy.

Gingko Biloba- Provides inner balance. Promotes the acceptance of all life.

Ginseng- Excellent stress remedy.

Gladiola- Good for training and learning, helps in assimilating information.

Golden Ear Drops- Aids in the release of deep sorrow.

Goldenrod- Excellent for animals who have been disempowered from abuse and lack of respect. For loss of will and soul.

Goldenseal- Excellent for all nervous system imbalances as well as behavioral problems. Removes scars from old emotional trauma.

Gotu Kola- A powerful overall tonic for all systems.

Gorse- Indicated for lethargy and lack of motivation.

Grape- Promotes love and devotion. Deeply emotionally supportive.

Grapefruit- Releases tensions. Promotes telepathy between humans and aquatic animals. Relieves training stress. Eases head and jaw stress.

Grape Hyacinth- Aids in the release of trauma and panic. Provides peace during stress.

Grass of Parnassus- Cleanses and recharges the energy fields, especially after surgery, illness or trauma. Maintains balance in crowded or polluted environments.

Green Bells of Ireland- Provides excellent support for the newborn. Wonderful for indoor animals. Restores heart and physical body connection to the Earth and enhances opening to the light and intelligence of nature.

Green Bog Orchid- Good for indoor animals. Opens energy flow to heart, releases constriction.

Green Fairy Orchid- Cleanses and opens energy to the heart. Allows attunement to the oneness of creation.

Grove Sandwort- Promotes the nurturing bond between newborn and mother. Increases awareness of nurturance from nature. Helps adapt to new surroundings more quickly. Enhances communication.

Gum Plant- A good relationship enhancer. Promotes bonding at the spiritual and soul level.

Hairy Butterwort- Indicated for behavioral difficulties, learning lessons the hard way. Allays stubbornness.

Harebell- Excellent remedy for group harmony. Opens the heart to universal love, dispelling fears that come with new family members of not enough love to go around. Promotes joy.

Hawthorne- Provides a perfect balance of love and peace for the heart. Provides emotional balance.

Heather- Relieves loneliness. Good for animals who spend a lot of time alone.

Hedgehog Cactus- Excellent for withdrawal and alienation from life. Provides nurturance, acceptance, confidence, comfort and balance. Especially for cats and rodents.

81

Heliconia- Enhances the balance of the left and right brain. Strengthens brain and spine.

Helleborous (Black)- Excellent for loss and transition. Helps to adjust gracefully to new circumstances. Promotes acceptance of change.

Henbane- Assists animals to transition into death.

Henna- Good during times of stress and transition. Provides divine support during major change.

Hibiscus- Excellent for nervous system calming. Alleviates stress. Provides strength and calm. Restorative.

Holly- Indicated for jealousy, anger and unprovoked attack, aggressive and mean-spirited behavior. Opens heart to the inpouring of love. Dispels fear of lack. Also for fever, coughing, respiratory stress. Eases pain and inflammation. Good in treatment of tumors.

Hollyhock- Good for indoor animals. Assists in attuning to the joy of the devic realm, and with angels who carry the quality of love. Excellent with Elements and Inert Gases.

Honeysuckle- Good for the loss of home or loved one. Aids grief and depression that are caused by loss.

Hooded Ladies Tresses- Excellent for release of deep cellular trauma. Very good for injury, abuse and neglect.

Hoptree- Provides boundary protection from environmental and human toxicity.

Hops- Promotes group harmony.

Hornbeam- Provides strength. Alleviates runny nose and sneezing. Eases morning tiredness. Transforms the loss of will to live and thrive. Uplifts depression.

Horseradish- Indicated for lethargy, depression and apathy. Provides alertness, clarity and vigor.

Horsetail- Assists in communication with higher energies, and the guides of human companions. For mild shock or trauma.

Hyssop- For co-dependence and boundary issues. Assists animals, especially cats, to not take on human disease and stress into their body. Promotes forgiveness to heal any hurt or memory between animals and humans. For cancers originating in guilt.

Icelandic Poppy- Opens receptivity to life, warmth and radiance.

Indian Pipe- Balances the flow of energy between the chakras. Excellent for back stress and strain.

Inmortal- Heals the trauma of abuse that results in depression, low self-esteem and shame. Excellent for dogs. Restores confidence, grace and heart healing.

Iris- Provides enthusiasm for life.

Impatiens- Helps agitation and nervousness. Restores patience and tolerance for difficult situations. Aids weight loss.

Jacob's Ladder- Eases anxiety, stubbornness and difficulties in relationship. Heart opener.

Jade- Brings growth and healing through release and letting go.

Jade Vine- Promotes heart-centered communication, particularly between animals and people.

Jasmine- Strengthens self-esteem. Useful for aromatherapy enhancement. Clears respiratory congestion from chest and sinuses. Balances digestive and respiratory systems.

Jerusalem Artichoke- Alleviates anger and moodiness. Provides emotional balance and support.

Jimson Weed- Provides alignment to guides, angelic and devic support. Promotes communion with nature. Good for sound therapies.

Jojoba- Indicated for aloofness and alienation from others due to hypersensitivity. Brings security, ease and comfort. Provides strength and a sense of belonging. Excellent relationship essence. Aromatherapy enhancer.

Jumping Cholla Cactus- Alleviates panic, frenzy, distraction and lack of focus. Gently provides balance and focus.

Kamani- Great heart healer, especially from trauma. Cleansing essence for all in the home.

Khat- Excellent for lethargy and apathy. Gives support and inspiration.

Kidney Bean- Alleviates hidden fears and anger. Excellent for kidney disease.

Kiwi- Eases fear, stress and moodiness. Provides emotional support from lack of love.

Klein's Pencil Cholla Cactus- For terminal animals who cannot release into death. Provides trust and support through transition. Brings freedom to release loved ones and move on with peace and joy.

Labrador Tea- Provides balance after trauma. Frees stress from extreme circumstances and behaviors, and from travel.

Ladies Slipper- Assists in opening to receive, stabilize and circulate energy flow into the body. Indicated for foot problems. For lack of self-nurturing. Provides mothering and support.

Ladies Tresses- Excellent for the release of trauma held deeply in body, increasing energy and interest in life. Provides joy and nurturance.

Larch- For low self-esteem. Alleviates fear.

Larkspur- Fosters group harmony. Promotes friendliness, courage, balance and good attitude.

Lavender- Enhances bonding and telepathic communion. Inspires confidence.

Lemon- Assists animals in training.

Lemon Balm- Aligns emotional and etheric bodies.

Lemmon's Paintbrush- Good for group harmony, communication and understanding.

Lettuce- Provides peace and calm.

Licorice- Good for hyperactivity. Provides calm. Excellent tranquilizer. Good for travel and any stressful situations.

Lilac- Excellent remedy for epilepsy, as well as neurological and spinal problems. Aligns chakras. Restores physical flexibility. Amplifies other remedies. Enhances telepathy.

Lily of the Valley- Eases the fear of dying.

Lime- Cleanses and opens the energy system.

Lima Bean- Indicated for foot problems by increasing the energy flow through feet. Grounding.

Lion's Tail- Good for group interactions and communication with proper boundaries. Promotes self-esteem.

Live Forever- Assists animals who are highly sensitive.

Lobelia- Excellent epilepsy remedy. Good for inflammatory conditions. For grieving manifesting as asthma, congestion or respiratory distress. Helps to target the underlying causes of disease. Releases trauma. Provides emotional balance.

Lobivia Cactus- Opens the heart to receive Christ energy. Grounding.

Locust- Provides support during difficult times. Aids in the animals evolution.

Loquat- Alleviates fear and anxiety. Good stress remedy. Eases travel.

Lotus- Use sparingly. For treatment of trauma and abuse. Assists opening of the heart. Increases attunement to higher psychic energies. Balances all energy centers. Enhances all other therapies, especially vibrational. Lends strength and grace during adversity. Excellent for recovery from surgery, especially spay and neutering. Brings emotional balance.

Love Lies Bleeding- For wounded, traumatized and suffering animals that have lost the will to live. Restores faith, hope and perseverance.

Luffa- For animals that have been in kennels, pound, cages, vet stays, etc. Rejuvenates and cleanses the entire being. Good for skin problems.

Lungwort- Indicated for post-op recovery. Increases the life energy in the body, especially in combination with eucalyptus. Good for trauma recovery.

Macadamia- Excellent for dissolving blockages that hold repeated negative behavior in place. Brings clarity. Balances emotions. Good for group harmony. Promotes communication and bonding.

Macartney Rose- Aids chronic fatigue. Assists relationship issues with humans.

Madia- For scatteredness and lack of focus, especially for cats. Excellent for training, particularly with horses.

Magnolia- Excellent essence for birth and death: a transition essence.

Mala Mujer- Excellent remedy for birth, and lack of maternal instincts. Indicated for emotional and nervous tension. Good for cats. Frees emotional expression, enhances maternal and feminine qualities.

Mallow- Strengthening and calming. Good for insecurity and anxiety. Attunes animals to the heart energy of God. Regenerating for aging and elderly animals. Alleviates the pain and fear of the aging process.

Maltese Cross- For emotional stress that comes from sudden loss, abandonment or trauma. Restores confidence in God.

Manzanita- For emotional balance, especially extreme shyness. Opens communication. Excellent for cats or wild animals in captivity. Indicated for hunger strikes and anorexic tendencies.

Maple- Opens the heart to give and receive unconditional love. Excellent for relationships.

Marigold (French)- Aids in learning and training, and the ability to absorb new information.

Mariposa Lily- Mothering remedy for pregnant and nursing animals. Heals damage from improper mothering, abandonment, and early separation. Provides the support of Mother God. May bring mild healing crisis as wounds heal. An excellent remedy for abuse, alienation, neglect and abandonment history. Also indicated for post-op recovery, especially spay and neutering procedures. For mistrust of love, warmth and security. For young animals in new home.

Marjoram- Supports the emotional body.

Meadowsweet- A nurturing, sweet essence. Provides unconditional love, promotes self-esteem. Excellent for trauma recovery.

Melaleuca- Good for group harmony. Opens the communication from the heart.

Melon Loco- Aids emotional congestion and restriction. Alleviates confusion and disconnectedness. Provides, balance, relaxation and grounding.

Mesquite- For alienation and aloofness due to trauma and abuse. Especially for cats. Facilitates forgiveness and reconnection to Source and self-value. Opens communication. Also good for indoor or captive wild animals who are not being exposed to nature.

Mezereum- Indicated for sadness, shyness and insecurity. Improves self-esteem issues. Opens the heart.

Milkmaids- Good for grumpiness, agitation and aloofness. Brings sweetness, love and acceptance of self.

Milkweed- Indicated for grief, despair and trauma. Gives support and emotional distance from stress.

Milky Nipple Cactus- For mother/infant bonding issues, disassociation, neediness and over-dependency. Provides nurturance, comfort and calm.

Milo- Excellent for animals who have been in the pound, in kennels or vet hospitals. Restorative.

Mimulus- Alleviates irrational fear and anxiety. Restores courage. Good for shyness and nervousness, especially with horses. Assists light sensitivity from injury or disease.

Monkeyflower Bush (Sticky Monkeyflower)- Assists with emotional cleansing.

Monkey Tail- Cleanses all systems in the body.

Monkshood- Indicated for abuse recovery. Helps animals to release fear of other animals stemming from past abuse. Heals soul wounding from abuse.

Monvillea Cactus- Indicated for breast and genital disorders.

Morning Glory- Excellent for the nervous system. Aids behavior disorders, such as overeating, inappropriate elimination, lethargy and excessive sleeping. Can break bad habits. Eases aggressive behavior that is fear based. Provides peace and trust. Promotes physical stamina and mental clarity.

Moschatel- Good for indoor animals. Promotes intuitive connection with plant realm.

Motherwort- Excellent for wild and captive sea and water creatures, coastal animals and indoor animals. Improves communication with devic spirits, particularly of the water. Greater understanding of relationship to plants, animals and the land. Aids in finer attunement to geopathic zones.

Mountain Pennyroyal- Provides psychic protection from toxic energy from humans and the environment.

Mountain Pride- For indoor animals and animals who have weak connection to their sexual nature and the Earth.

Mountain Wormwood- Promotes forgiveness. Release of resentment and old wounds towards self or others.

Mugwort- Relaxing. Eases the longing heart. Calms anxiety and fear. Helps animals to attune to the angelic realms in their sleep. Excellent for puppies in a new home.

Mulberry (Red)- Allays grief and mourning. Restores vitality and purpose. Helps to attune to group consciousness.

Mullein- Excellent remedy to assist in training. Provides focus. For fatigue and lack of endurance, indecisiveness. Provides vibrancy and self-assuredness.

Mushroom- Allays stubbornness, inflexibility and nervous behavior. Assists horses in training. Aids release of trauma from injury, poor treatment and abuse.

Mustard- Alleviates depression and despair. Invites divine grace and hope. Fosters compassion.

Nectarine- Indicated for anger as well as withdrawal. Alleviates emotional extremes.

Noble Star Flower Cactus- Provides supportive love energies and a greater understanding of the consequences of eating smaller prey.

Noni- For mother/young related issues, heart-related stress or wounding. Provides loving support from the heart of Mother God. Good birth essence. Purifies and detoxes.

Northern Ladies Slipper- Excellent trauma and abuse remedy. Good for difficult birth experiences. Gently releases trauma held deeply in the body and opens pathways to pervasive healing. Enhances body/soul fusion. For those who resist healing and feel unsupported by life.

Oak- Eases despondency, despair and stress. Empowers self-esteem, especially after neglect, abuse or abandonment. Fosters patience, stamina, perseverance and acceptance. Eases abdominal and digestive tension.

Ocotillo- Alleviates anger from buried wounds of abuse and trauma. Excellent for horses. Soothes reactive, gut aggression. Soothing, calming and grounding. Opens heart to unconditional love.

Ohi'a Lehua- Assists attunement to the earth. Useful for animals who are shifting from predator diet to more vegetarian.

Okra- Alleviates stress in group situations. Grounding.

Old Maid- Good post-trauma remedy. Promotes acceptance and forgiveness of those that have caused harm.

Oleander- Provides deep emotional release.

Olive- Builds strength and gives comfort in sickness, exhaustion and trauma. For lethargy and tiredness from anemia.

One-Sided Wintergreen- Provides psychic support and protection for the highly sensitive animal. Strengthens boundaries and fosters group harmony with people or animals.

Onion- Cleanses emotional trauma and pain. Releases fear of separation, birth trauma, mother/young bonding and separation issues. Cleanses the entire system. Good flea remedy.

Orange- Promotes joy. Aids in release of obsessive behaviors. Calming.

Orange Flame Flower Cactus- Releases anger, promotes self-forgiveness. Excellent for horses that have been abused or traumatized, that display angry or withdrawn behavior.

Orchid- Good for recovery from spay and neuter surgery. Balances all bodies and emotions, especially in highly stressful situations.

Oregon Grape Root- Transforms hostility to trust. Calms wild and captive animals. Releases over-dependency and neediness. Promotes self-love. Opens the heart to trust.

Pansy (Heartsease)- Supreme anti-viral remedy. Indicated for HIV and leukemia. Alleviates grief and pain from the trauma of abuse. Allows trust and healing on all levels. Excellent for recovery from spay and neutering procedures. Cleansing.

Papaya- Strengthens and energizes all systems.

Parsley- Powerful balancer of the energy systems.

Partridgeberry- Enhances the relationships between animals and humans.

Passion Flower- Allows access to higher psychic energies. Provides divine support. Good for emotional chaos. Heals the heart, and provides love and joy. Relaxing and comforting in the highest sense.

Paw Paw- Improves self-esteem. Aids in nutrient assimilation from food.

Peach- Alleviates depression that accompanies debilitating immune system diseases. Also for animals who are light sensitive. Speeds up healing time.

Peanut- Eases stress and deep fears. Good for kidney problems.

Pear- Promotes peacefulness. Good for group harmony. Excellent essence to use with sound healing.

Pecan- Balances emotions.

Penstemon- First-aid remedy for abuse, illness or trauma. Provides stamina, courage and inner strength. Relieves overwhelm and self-doubt.

Pennyroyal- Supreme essence for psychic protection. Aids in release of trauma.

Peony- Beautiful provider of the loving aspects of Mother God. Opens the heart, restores self-esteem and communication. Excellent for recovery of any kind, neutering and spaying procedures in particular.

Periwinkle- Provides lightness of being. Gently yet powerfully lifts deep and chronic depression and disassociation. Grounding, balancing and inspiring.

Pine- Alleviates sustained guilt from "bad" behavior or abuse. Good for puppies in training. Provides upliftment and joy. Promotes forgiveness of self and others.

Pine Drops- Rids the body of antibiotics and drugs from surgical procedures.

Pineapple- Promotes self-assuredness. Powerful chakra balancer and enhancer.

Pineapple Weed- Promotes the nurturing bond between newborn and mother, as well as nurturance from nature. For disconnectedness to the Earth and accident-prone behavior.

Pink Laurel- Deeply comforting for animals that do not feel at home on Earth. Relaxing. Purifies the blood. Assists body/soul fusion.

Pink Monkeyflower- Eases shame after abuse or trauma. Allows reconnection to God. Improves self-esteem.

Pink Powder Puff- Assists attunement to subtle energies, particularly for healing. Awakens loving heart energy flow.

Pink Tecoma- Very nurturing and comforting. Provides a sense of security and optimism.

Pitcher Plant- Helps domestic animals to stop preying on smaller animals for food.

Plantain- Indicated for behavior patterns that have become frozen from fear or abuse. Provides release and calm, allowing a lighter and gentler experience.

Pleurisy Root- Alleviates stress and anxiety from suppressed rage and grief from abuse and trauma. Excellent for horses. Eases all abandonment and mothering issues.

Plumbago- Alleviates emotional lethargy. Restores loving vitality to individuals in family settings. Promotes group harmony.

Poha- Heals the emotional scarring from difficult relationship issues. Eases emotional lethargy. Enhances all training regimens.

Poison Ivy- Eases irritability and anxiety. Provides calm and balance. Strengthening.

Poke Weed- Alleviates depression. Emotional balancer.

Pomegranate- Excellent mothering essence. Provides nurturance and self-confidence. Heals unresolved early-life traumas from lack of mothering.

Potato- Allows physical release of issues held deeply in body. Increases the ability to receive love and acceptance.

Prickly Pear Cactus- Provides adaptability and calm.

Prickly Wild Rose- Eases lethargy. Restores interest in life. Aids in trust and openness to others.

Prickly Poppy- Promotes deep forgiveness.

Pukiawe- Excellent for outdoor animals. Restores the connection to nature, the Earth and all of life.

Purple Nightshade- Alleviates pain and nervousness. Excellent nervous system tonic. Calms and soothes.

Quaking Grass- Promotes group harmony and bonding. Eases territorial issues. Excellent for kennel and pound animals. An excellent essence for vets to use in their offices.

Queen Anne's Lace- For fear and mistrust. Attunes animals to higher psychic energies. Transmutes trauma to joy. Excellent for emotional wounding. Assists in the severing of psychic ties and misplaced loyalties. Promotes self-esteem. Boosts the immune system.

Queen of the Night- Excellent for abandonment and abuse, and being disconnected from life. Indicated for hopelessness, scatteredness, fear and alienation. Provides radiance and integration. Restores receptivity and feeling. Emotionally grounding.

Quinoa- Very grounding.

Rabbitbrush- Excellent essence for the anxious and high-strung animal, either by genetic predisposition or breed. Brings ease and flow.

Radish- Increases the life force.

Raspberry- Promotes kindness and open-heartedness.

Rattlesnake Plantain Orchid- Lifts aggression and anger. Excellent for horses.

Red Bud (Judas Tree)- Indicated for grief and depression. Restores the will to live after trauma, injury or abuse.

Red Mountain Heather- Enhances the effects of essences, energy medicine of any kind, and music.

Red Rugosa Rose- Stabilizing and balancing during times of transition and stress.

Redwood- Excellent for death and transition, loss and grief. Renews faith in life and her processes. Opens animals to unconditional love. Excellent for urinary tract disorders of any kind.

Rhododendron- Eases the fear of travel.

Rice- Eases high stress, especially affecting the kidneys and skin. Alleviates hidden fears, and issues around discipline.

River Beauty- Excellent for shock, trauma and abuse. Heals the emotional body after sudden loss of loved one. Releases tension from the physical body. Regenerating.

Robinia- Relieves lethargy and inertia. Provides life spark.

Rock Rose- Indicated for dehydration with vomiting and diarrhea. Good for panic.

Rosa Buff Beauty- Aids group dynamics. Opens the heart to group interaction.

Rosa Christata- Promotes tissue regeneration.

Rosa Corymbifera- Releases stress held in head, neck and shoulders.

Rosa Gallica Officinalis- Alleviates depression, stress, and emotional shutdown. Opens the heart to joy. Excellent enhancer of other essences.

Rosa Hardii- For indoor and light deprived animals. Good for trauma recovery. Promotes attunement to devas and the sun. Connects to Inner Light and joy.

Rosa Horrida- Primary essence to assist the animal realm in forgiveness of humans. Good for tissue regeneration.

Rosa Macrantha- Releases blockages in the energy body.

Rosa Macrophylla- Queen of all rose essences. Opens the heart center to divine love and beauty. Excellent for healing of all abuse and trauma. Restores faith in God. Opens the ability to heal.

Rosa Mutabilis- Helps animals to track and stay in step with the accelerating human evolution and frequency shifts on the Planet.

Rosa Nutkana- Indicated for post-trauma. Encourages loving relationship and healing from past hurt.

Rose- Provides enhanced attunement to higher psychic realms. Excellent remedy to assist after spay or neuter procedures.

Rosemary- Provides happiness and sensitivity.

Sacred Datura- First-aid remedy for shattered reality, sudden loss of loved one, extreme loneliness and depression. Indicated for soul loss. Eases confusion, gives courage and aids communication with psychic realms and those who have crossed over. Cleanses and rebalances chakras.

Sage- Cleanses the energy field.

Saguaro- Excellent remedy for delinquent and wild cats. Excellent for HIV. For abuse and surgery recovery. Rekindles the will to survive and heal, providing endurance, grounding, courage and determination. Promotes trust and stillness during transition.

Saint John's Wort- For poor boundaries, especially after abuse. Assists in letting in what is protective and nurturing, and clearing traumatic and destructive memories. Releases fear. Opens animal to spiritual, loving support and trust, while offering protection from environmental toxicity. Good for timid, shy animals.

Sandalwood- Opens the physical body's receptivity to aromatherapy oils and aids in their healing process.

Scarlet Runner Bean- Excellent for trauma, injury or shock. Dispels fear.

Scleranthus- Alleviates carsickness. Good for constipation. Eases low vitality and moodiness.

Scotch Broom- For unexplained suffering and depression. Indicated for soul loss.

Screw Pine- Good for allergies.

Sea Lettuce- Aids in assimilation of water by the body. Can reduce free radical damage in the body. Excellent for rehydration after surgical procedures and all travel.

Self-Heal- A primary abuse remedy, also effective in sickness, injury and trauma. Restores vitality and radiant health. Connects each being to the Creator. Provides deep calm during trauma and stress. Indicated for all survival issues. Amplifies other remedies.

Sensitive Plant- For extreme introversion and shyness. Especially for cats. Eases stress.

Shasta Daisy- Excellent essence for the young. Good for mother and newborn bonding. Facilitates training, stimulates instinctive wisdom, and assists wild animals in retuning to the wild.

Shasta Lily- Excellent for mother and newborn. Provides nurturing love from the heart of Mother God. Excellent for babies, indoor animals, wild animals and animals in transition.

Shrimp Plant- Provides direct connection to angelic realm, particularly through whales and dolphins.

Shooting Star- For birth first aid. Allays alienation from life, home and family. Excellent for ferile animals.

Sierra Rein Orchid- Provides immediate relief from depression, sadness and suppressed emotions.

Single Delight- Provides support after a move or transition of any kind. Indicated for isolation and separation from mother, siblings and family group.

Sitka Burnet- Cleanses old energy patterns from the body. Good for training and learning.

Snapdragon- Supreme essence for mouth, throat, teeth, vocal chords and any aspects related to the throat chakra. Aligns cranial plates. Excellent for easing aggression that is focused through biting, growling, snarling, inappropriate chewing, grinding or eating disorders. Primary essence for lick granuloma. For dental problems, pre and post-op surgeries involving mouth, jaw, teeth or gums. For horses who have problems with bits.

Snowplant- Excellent essence for transition. Supports change, strengthens the aura and subtle bodies.

Soapberry- Helps animals release fear of other animals and nature. Excellent for indoor animals. Releases muscle tension around the heart.

Sorrel- Protects against emotional depletion in stressful situations.

Spanish Bayonet- Good physical cleanser, especially of heavy metals accumulated in city air.

Spider Lily- Strengthens digestive organs, sexual reproductive organs, kidneys, and the skin.

Spiderwort- Excellent cancer remedy.

Spirea- Provides nurturance for the newborn. Provides support from nature.

Spruce- Provides inner peace, light and joy.

Squash- Indicated for breeding, pregnancy and nursing mothers. Offers support after spay and neuter surgery. Grounding.

Staghorn Cholla Cactus- For extreme scatteredness and disassociation after transition or upheaval. Reintegrating. Restores calm, faith, focus and security.

Star of Bethlehem- Supreme remedy for shock, trauma and grief. Excellent for street animals, or those in shelters. Eases weaning. Assists recovery from all surgery. Excellent for treatment of trauma or abuse from other animals. Eases inflammation. Restores balance and calm. Especially for cats.

Star Tulip (Cat's Ears)- Excellent for epilepsy. Indicated for post-op recovery (especially spay and neuter procedures), trauma, abuse, overwhelm, anxiousness, withdrawal and disconnection from the body. Helps animals to ground. Alleviates the fear of death.

Stephanotis- For indoor and light deprived animals. Enhances absorption of sunlight. Increases awareness of subtle dimensions.

Stinging Nettle- Provides calmness and balance in family stress.

Strawberry- Restores dignity, especially after abuse or neglect. Restores will.

Sugar Cane- Alleviates emotional imbalance, lethargy and depression.

Summer Snowflake- Good for animals that live in areas of extreme seasonal and weather changes. Eases transition, as well as stress from travel.

Sunflower- Important remedy for indoor animals. Increases vitality by aiding the ability to receive energy from the sun. Alleviates fatigue. Strengthens sense of being in the world. Balances extreme behaviors. Good for spay and neuter post-op. Cleanses the heart center.

Swamp Onion- Cleanses psychic debris from the subtle bodies. Opens all bodies to the loving, cleansing energy of God.

Sweet Briar- Excellent remedy for hopelessness, when trauma and abuse have occurred. Heals the heart. Excellent for wild animals.

Sweet Chestnut- For animals who are deeply exhausted.

Sweet Flag- Indicated for anxiety and fear of transition. Integrates mind, body and spirit. Enhances other flower remedies.

Sweetgale- Assists in the healing of relationships, especially inappropriate over-dependency and emotional attachment to others.

Sweetgrass- For shock and trauma. Regenerates and purifies the etheric body and immediate environment.

Sweet Chestnut- Eases suffering from exhaustion.

Sweet Pea- Good for group harmony. Fosters bonding, love and trust, especially after abuse. Relieves wandering. For cats who are aloof. Calms the emotional body.

Sycamore- For stagnation and lethargy. Provides gentle and joyous support. Eases stress.

Tagua- Promotes direct connection to guardian angels. Excellent for elephants in sanctuary and recovery, providing peace and awareness.

Tansy- Excellent for psychic protection and change. Repels negative thought-forms. Changes or eliminates the effects of psychic attack.

Tea Plant- Alleviates lethargy and stagnation. Provides creative spark.

Tea Tree- Opens the heart and energy centers. Enhances the affects of acupuncture.

Teddy Bear Cholla Cactus- Indicated for self-esteem issues arising from shame and deep fear, resulting in bonding and communication issues. Heart healer. Promotes peace and contentment.

Thistle- Strengthens boundaries. Good for group harmony.

Thurber's Gilia- Good for traumatic transition, fear and insecurity. Provides assistance in moving through fear into strength and empowerment.

Thyme- Regulates the endocrine system.

Tiger Lily- Transmutes aggressive and hostile tendencies in animals (especially cats) to curiosity and playfulness. Resolves underlying fear. For inappropriate elimination. Promotes harmony in relationship, one to one and in groups. Restores balance and trust. Good for spay and neuter post-op.

Tobacco- Good for blocks in energetic bodies. Improves effects of acupuncture and acupressure. Assists animals in learning. Provides calm for animals transiting into death.

Tomato- Provides strength and courage. Anti-viral and anti-bacterial. Boosts the immune system. Develops patience. Very cleansing. Apply directly on wounds and abscesses.

Tree of Life- Eases depression.

Tree Opuntia- Good for animals who are elderly or resistant to change. Supports them through transition.

Tree Peony- Indicated for any relationship issues. Promotes unconditional love and the experience of the oneness of all life.

Trillium- Provides centering and peace.

True Wood Sorrel- Provides centering amid chaotic environmental conditions.

Trumpet Vine- Strong strengthener of the energy system. Enhances the effect of vibrational remedies. Encourages self-assertiveness and individual personality in family groups.

Tuberose- Enhances the affects of aromatherapy.

Tundra Twayblade- Heals abuse and trauma. Releases chaos, confusion and constriction from the heart, presenting as withdrawal and aloofness. Provides unconditional love.

Uala- For shock, anger and trauma recovery. Emotionally balancing. Restores communication.

Valerian- Indicated for stress and hyperactivity.

Vervain- Relaxes high-strung animals (particularly dogs) who are nervous and overactive, especially barking and jumping behavior.

Vine- Specifically for the territorial animal who is dominating and aggressive. Excellent for wolves and headstrong horses.

Vitex- Excellent for all animals for absorption and assimilation of minerals, especially after ill health or compromised living conditions.

Waikiki Rainbow Cactus- Enhances self-esteem.

Wallflower- Develops individuality in group dynamics. Overcomes lethargy. Stimulates joy and restores confidence.

Walnut- Assists emotional adjustment to new circumstances and behaviors. Aids transition with animals and people. Provides calm and peace. Fosters heart communication. Excellent birth essence, especially for sickness following delivery. Good for the aloof feline.

Water Violet- For overly independent, shy or aloof animals who are disconnected to those around them. For grumpy and unresponsive dogs. Promotes self-forgiveness and forgiveness of others.

Weeping Willow- Eases emotional numbness during crisis or loss. Supports movement through grief into healing. Eases reconnection to the emotional body.

Whitethorn- Indicated for behavior and training issues. Good for nervous tension and exhaustion. Assists in breaking negative patterns of behavior. Provides calm, clarity and flow.

White Chestnut- For anxiety and nervousness. Excellent training essence. Aids in the release of old behaviors.

White Fireweed- For emotional shock and trauma, especially from abuse. Releases emotional pain, relieves alienating behavior from prior abuse.

White Violet- Provides support for the newborn. Protects the super-sensitive. For trust issues, insecurity, and claustrophobic tendencies.

Wild Ginger- Provides zest and spark to animals who are lethargic, uninspired and stuck in a rut.

Wild Oat- Indicated for scatteredness and lack of connection to the body and world. For conditions that will not respond to treatment. Good for depression from boredom and being indoors. Excellent for retired rescue and show animals. Good for birds who pick at their feathers.

Wild Rose- Indicated for loss of interest, indifference and apathy towards life. Sparks the love of life. For unexplained worsening conditions.

Wild Sweet Pea- Indicated for trauma, abuse and surgery recovery. Also promotes group harmony. Increases inner sense of strength, security and confidence. Good for animals who wander and have a lost sense of home.

Willow- Effective in alleviating resentment arising out of feeling unappreciated, or feeling that she/he was being treated wrongfully. For oversensitivity, on all levels, including allergies.

Wintergreen- Provides support for animals with poor boundaries and lack of confidence. Uplifting and energizing.

Wisteria (Chinese)- Balances the subtle bodies. Strengthens the energetic system. Useful in acupuncture and massage. Alleviates flea and mite problems.

Wolfberry- Good first-aid formula for transition, loss, grief, deep sadness and overwhelm. Provides security at the core levels.

Wood Betony- Balances sexual energies after spaying and neutering. Helpful for animals that wander.

Wormwood- Eases negative thought-form and energetic bombardment from people. Provides psychic protection.

Woven Spine Pineapple Cactus- Good remedy for trauma, abuse and abandonment, resulting in lack of will to live. Relieves deep exhaustion. Releases deep blockages of the life-force. Provides self-esteem and courage.

Yarrow- Provides psychic protection, release of trauma, assistance during stress, and friction between the human family. An excellent remedy for animals who are highly sensitive, and absorb the ills of their humans into their own bodies.

Yellow Dryas- For animals who feel alone, unsupported and isolated from their soul family.

Yerba Mate- Excellent for training and learning. Enhances memory and attention span.

Yerba Santa- Excellent shock and trauma remedy. Remedies emotional extremes. Good for pound and kennel animals, vet visits, travel in carriers, etc. Balances fear and hysteria from these experiences. Relieves stress disorders. Good for epilepsy, hysteria, immune system compromise, and lick granuloma.

Ylang Ylang- Relieves anger, depression, frustration and tension. Good stress remedy. Restores balance after travel.

Yucca- Excellent for anger and loss of will from trauma, injury or sickness. Indicated for fear and despair. Provides steadfastness. Unifies courage and will.

Zinnia- Lifts tension and stress. Aligns all bodies. Uplifting at the heart level.

Zucchini- Provides energy, strength and stamina.

Gem Elixirs

Gem elixirs have a special relationship with the animal realm. Working more closely with the physical body than other vibrational remedies, these tinctures are keenly attuned to the creatures of nature, and work intimately in concert with them. Elixirs made from gemstones also affect the other levels of being, but in animals the relationship is unique.

Throughout time, many ancient cultures utilized and understood the powerful healing influence of gems, crystals and their essences. They were used in ancient Tibet, China, Egypt, India, and by the Aztecs, Mayans and indigenous peoples around the globe, as well as in Lemuria and Atlantis.

As with the preparation of flower essences, gem elixirs are made by placing the stone in pure water in bright morning sunlight or moonlight. The morning is best for sunlight because the life energy of the sun is strongest then. The specific energetic signature of the crystal or gemstone is solar or lunar infused into the water, and later mixed with equal parts alcohol (vodka or grain alcohol is usually used for gems). This energetically infused water and alcohol is the mother tincture. As with the creation of all mother essences, the purest, highest and most reverent attitude is necessary for the correct fusion and transference to occur.

Gem elixirs vary somewhat from flower essences because of the energy of the molecular structure of the crystal or gemstone. The physical body, whether animal or human, contains crystalline structure throughout—in the blood and brain, neurological tissue, spine and vertebrae. Scientists have recently discovered that the key to birds inner knowing of migration seasons and routes may be triggered by a magnetic component in their brains, orienting them to the correct direction at the precise season, and even day of the year.

97

Gem and mineral elixirs carry many minerals as part of their physical signatures. This can aid in the absorption and assimilation of minerals by the body. The gem tinctures carry the profoundly stable energetic pattern, or grid of the gemstone. This stabilizing affect can be very valuable for animals, who are keenly attuned to the world of rocks and the Earth, or who are deprived from this natural relationship due to being kept indoors. The addition of gem elixirs to flower and starlight combinations can be very beneficial. It can ground, stabilize and give depth to the entire blend, and the natural complement of stones, stars and flowers can amplify all of the individual essences.

Gem Elixir Qualities

Acharandite- Aids circulation in the physical body. Supports thyroid and adrenal function.

Aegerine- Improves circulation and the blood by deepening the connection between the root chakra and circulatory system.

Agate (Botswana)- Provides upliftment. Excellent for lethargy and depression.

Agate (Carnelian)- For extreme stress and fatigue. Opens the body's ability to access the life force.

Agate (Fire)- Excellent for use in color therapy.

Agate (Moss)- An excellent remedy for depression, especially due to light and nature deprivation. Aids assimilation of nutrients.

Alexandrite- Aids self-confidence, lethargy and depression. Especially for indoor animals. Good for color therapy.

Amethyst- Restores self-confidence after abuse or abandonment. For the shy and withdrawn animal. Promotes group harmony.

Anapoite- Balances, calms and soothes the energy bodies.

Antimony- Alleviates fear. Strengthens the emotional body.

Apophyllite- For indoor animals. Helps animals to attune to nature.

Aquamarine- Good for trauma recovery, especially when the animal is fearful and disoriented. Uplifting.

Artinite- An important essence for indoor animals who are light deprived. Enhances light absorption from sunlight, light healing and energy healing. Brings light frequencies into the DNA. Promotes deep peace.

Atacamite- Good essence for alleviating stress.

Aventurine- Provides strength and stamina during stressful new experiences. For fear of the unknown. Cleanses the subtle bodies.

Azurite- Good for arthritis.

Azurite/Malachite- Alleviates anxiety and compulsive behaviors.

Barite- Transforms hostility, aggression, anger and fear. Brings enthusiasm. Excellent for abused and traumatized horses.

Beaudantite- Promotes love and forgiveness through the understanding of different species. Brings peace.

Berthierite- Opens channels of circulation to the feet, legs and knees from the Earth. Cleansing to the blood.

99

Beryl- Good for all conditions involving the jaw, mouth and throat.

Beryl (Red)- Strengthens the root chakra, legs, knees and feet. Eases deep survival issues.

Bismuth- Assists in clearing radiation from the physical body.

Bloodstone- Allays emotional lethargy. Eases resistance to being grounded in the body. Good for all blood disorders.

Brass- Cleanses the physical body.

Bronze- Aids in mineral and nutrient absorption. Indicated for leukemia.

Broshentite- Excellent remedy for group harmony. Promotes acceptance, trust and a sense of belonging. Grounding.

Brucite- For abuse and trauma history. Restores connection with God and the beauty of life.

Calcite (Cobaltian)- Enhances mineral absorption. Bone strengthener.

Calcite (Orange)- Important essence for indoor animals. Aids in depression from light deprivation. Increases the ability to receive energy from the sun. For lethargy and lack of creative spark. Aids kidney function. Bone strengthener.

Callaghanite- For clearing of blockages in the heart on all levels. Clears energy upwardly, through the heart chakra. Restores balanced emotions and expression.

Carletonite- For anxiety and hyperactivity. Provides deep relaxation. Good with sound healing.

Cassiterite- Alleviates fear, anger and hatred.

Cavanisite- Brings lightness, joy and wonder. Excellent for recovery.

Celestite- Good communication essence.

Chabazite- Assists in shifting negative energy out of the body before it manifests as disease. Aids in sound healing.

Chalcedony- Eases all birth difficulties for mother and babies. Indicated for leukemia.

Chromium- Aids in the utilization of calcium, silica, magnesium, potassium and sodium.

Chrysocolla- Heart opener. Lifts unresolved grief, trauma and stress. Good for long distance travel.

Chrysolite- Cleanses and detoxes the physical body.

Chyrsoprase- For indoor animals. Restores balance between the heart and the Earth. Helps animals to feel at home in nature. Cleanses heart of chaos and pain. Good for aggression. Promotes group harmony.

Clay- Pulls toxicity from all body systems.

Clinoclase- Assists in giving and receiving love. Promotes forgiveness.

Clinoptilolite- For transition of any kind. Helps to hold a focus of love and peace during change. Eases physical tension, especially in neck and shoulders.

Cobaltite- Aids in the ability to absorb life force (prana) into the body through water. Excellent for fish, dolphins, whales and all sea creatures. A good remedy to be used with aromatherapy.

Copper- Eases inflammation. Helps ease fear of death for terminal or aging animals.

Coral (Black)- Alleviates blockages in the lower chakras, especially survival issues, birth trauma and abuse. Excellent for the spine and lower back. Excellent for bones.

Coral (Purple)- Excellent remedy to aid cranial-sacral therapy.

Coral (Red)- For back stress and spinal problems. Also aids in weight loss. Attunes animals to other animals, people and nature. Strengthens the physical heart. Good for the elderly. Excellent for bones.

Covellite- Provides protection from overload. Especially for highly sensitive animals with poor boundaries.

Crocoite- Grounds and opens the root chakra. Relaxing.

Cuproskowdilite- For regeneration, especially after surgery or severe stress. Good for kennel and cage stress.

Datolite- For animals who have recently lost a loved one. Aids in communication with beings who have passed over.

Diaboleite- Cleanses the emotional body of negative images held by fear.

Diamond (Pink)- Opens the heart to ecstatic love. Gives divine emotional support.

Diamond (White)- Detoxes and purifies all bodies. Balances the brain.

Dioptase- Relieves stress and tension from sudden change.

Duftite- Alleviates stuck attitudes and behavior patterns.

Dumortierite- Relieves stress from travel and separation from home environment.

Durangite- Excellent stress remedy.

Eilat Stone- Regenerates tissue and bone.

Emerald- Excellent trauma essence. Provides heart support during loss and grief. Universal heart cleanser and balancer. Brings upliftment from nature.

Epistilbite- For abuse recovery. Indicated for anger and aggression.

Fluorite- Breaks up and releases blockages stored in energy field. For stagnation and congestion of energy on all levels. Purifying. Regenerates teeth and bone.

Garnet (Rhodolite)- Indicated for body/soul fusion. For animals who will not heal, especially after surgery or trauma. For disassociation. Grounding and regenerating.

Garnet (Spessartine)- Strengthens all aspects of the heart, physically and energetically.

Garnet (Tsavorite)- Reinforces healing energy. Good for recovery.

Glaucocerinite- Excellent remedy for breaking through extreme blockages held in place by fear.

Gold- Supreme heart opener and strengthener. Helps in the assimilation of gold into the body. Supports the nervous system. Purifies the physical body. Brings radiant joy and self-confidence.

Gordonite- Good essence for animals who are in training. Helps to assimilate new information.

Hancockite- Good for indoor animals. Promotes deeper connection to nature.

Hematite- Provides strength and protection in negative environments. Alleviates overwhelm. Good for all blood disorders.

Hemimorphite- Excellent remedy to use with sound healing.

Herderite- Alleviates extreme moods and behaviors.

Herkimer Diamond- Indicated for lethargy and loss of interest in life. Provides energy and zip. Releases stress and tension.

Heulandite- Opens the heart to give and receive love.

Ivory- Bone strengthener. Excellent training essence, especially for horses. Indicated for leukemia.

Jade- Excellent cleansing essence for the blood and all aspects of the physical body. Provides the openness to receive the highest frequency of love. Good with sound healing.

Jadeite- Calms emotional agitation and anxiety. For the nervous animal.

Jarosite- Strengthens deeper contact with the Earth. Centering and balancing for all animals.

Jasper (Green)- Excellent recovery essence after trauma, shock and surgery. Also very good for indoor animals, synchs internal body rhythms with cycles of the Planet. Grounding. Good for spay and neuter recovery. Accelerates healing on all levels. Increases the life force.

Jasper (Picture)- For the timid, shy and withdrawn animal. Especially for cats.

Jet- Calms all emotional states, particularly anxiety and depression. Good for stress.

Kasolite- Enhances joy in relationship. Good for group harmony.

Kinoite- Improves communication. Good for sound healing.

Krupkaite- For group harmony. Provides deep attunement with the Earth. Excellent for circulatory, muscle and skeletal systems.

Kunzite (Pink)- Energizing and healing to the heart on all levels. Uplifting and inspiring. Emotionally warming.

Kunzite (White)- Opens receptivity to the angelic realm. Opens and supports the heart. Regenerating on all levels.

Kutnahorite- For the cleansing and strengthening of all bodies. Used with xenon inert gas, aids in skin, nerve, hair and skeletal growth.

Lapis Lazuli- Cleanser and strengthener. Excellent for all throat problems.

Larimar- For indoor animals. Aids in attuning to the Earth as a living Being.

Lazulite- Excellent for anger, hostility and frustration. Especially good for horses.

Lepidolite- Balances extreme emotional states.

Libethenite- For grieving and depressed animals. Clears emotional blocks. Brings peace and beauty.

Lodestone (Negative/Positive)- Very balancing. Excellent for animals in training—aids in assimilating information.

Magnesium- Physical heart strengthener.

Malachite- Good for indoor animals. Grounds connection to the physical world. For weak body soul connection. Aligns all bodies.

Manganese- Aids in the absorption of iron.

Mesolite- Good group harmony essence. Promotes love for oneself and others.

Mixite- Indicated for hip dysplasia. Energizes the legs, hips and heart. Brings energy into the body. Good for winter doldrums. Adds spark.

Moldavite- Provides grounding as well as expansion into greater dimensions of devic and angelic support.

Moonstone- For animals who are hypersensitive, stressed and emotionally out of balance. Provides centering and relaxed openness. Excellent birthing essence.

Nephrite- Excellent for detoxing and strengthening the kidneys.

Okenite- Helpful during transition. Balances and strengthens the energy body.

Opal- For post-op recovery. Energizes, soothes and regenerates the energy field. Provides clarity and balance. Good for lethargy.

Opal (Dark)- Good for neutering, spaying and all post-op recovery.

Pearl- For stress and irritability. Restores resilience.

Peridot- Provides support for the newborn, new growth, new cycles and living situations. Opens the heart. Cleansing and regenerating.

Petrified Wood- Physical heart strengthener.

Phenakite- Excellent for group harmony.

Philipsburgite- Helps heart energy to surface and be expressed. Excellent for hostile animals, especially horses. Combine with Ginkgo Biloba for the physical heart.

Platinum- Excellent for depression and lethargy. Lifts the spirits. Regenerates the heart. Excellent training essence.

Purpurite- Aids in sound healing.

Pyrite- Excellent remedy for stress and depression.

Pyromorphite- Good for indoor animals. Provides grounding and deep connection to the Earth. Excellent in sound healing.

Pyroxmangite- Opens the heart chakra to receive love. Resolves emotional issues.

Quartz (Brazilian)- For shock and weak body/soul link. Provides grounding and ease in adapting to new surroundings. Releases toxins from the energy field. Cleanses and energizes all bodies and fields.

Quartz (Citrine)- Excellent cleanser. Provides alignment with Mother nature. Good for indoor animals. Aids light deprivation.

Quartz (Rose)- Supreme heart cleanser and strengthener. Opens heart to receive love. Excellent for aggressive and hostile animals. Restores faith and self- esteem after abuse.

Quartz (Rutilated)- Regenerating. Eases sadness.

Quartz (Smoky)- Cleanses toxic energy from all aspects of being. Supportive for long distance travel. Uplifting. Eases sadness.

Quartz (White)- Balances emotional extremes. Calms the energetic bodies.

Quartzite- Alleviates clinginess and over-dependence in insecure animals.

Rhodochrosite- Opens the heart. Clears pain and confusion from heart. Regenerates epidermal tissue.

Ruby- Provides security at the core levels. Supreme heart healer, strengthener and balancer on all levels. Alleviates hostility, aggression and anger.

Sapphire- Excellent for birth trauma and abandonment. Eases depression and lethargy.

Sarabauite- Increases the ability to give and receive love. Excellent for trauma and abuse recovery. Resolves issues of abandonment.

Sarandite- Good for neutering recovery. Relieves anger stored in jaw. Excellent for horses. Enhances connection with the Earth.

Sardonyx- Relieves emotional extremes, particularly grief, depression and anxiety.

Scholzite- Excellent group harmony remedy, especially with new members of the family. Valuable in assisting with change and transition.

Silver- Supreme destressor. Strengthens the nervous system. Balances the energy system.

Sodalite- Strengthens the lymphatic system. Provides emotional balance.

Spectrolite- Indicated for lethargy. Recharges and soothes the energy field.

Star Sapphire- For animals that have been abused or abandoned. Restores trust in life. Balancing and aligning.

Strontianite- Aids in the absorption and utilization of calcium in the physical body.

Szenicsite- For lethargy, depression and inertia. Brings life, joy and strength into the body.

Tiger's Eye- For animals who are angry or jealous due to human abuse or trauma. Especially effective for ferile cats.

Tin- Aids in grief, loss and despair. Strengthens lungs and lung meridian.

Topaz- Releases blocks stored in the gut from past trauma and pain. Opens animals to Spirit. Balances extreme emotions. Aligns etheric and physical bodies. Tissue regenerator.

Torbernite- Stimulates the heart chakra. Brings peace and joy, with a deeper attunement to the angelic realm.

Tourmaline (Black)- Cleanses toxic energy from all aspects of being. Relieves stress and overwhelm. Aids long distance travel.

Tourmaline (Blue)- Aids communication, lessens barking.

Tourmaline (Chrome)- Assists in powerful opening of the heart chakra. Indicated for heart conditions and problems.

Tourmaline (Watermelon)- For animals who are unable to receive or give love. Eases and heals heart pain. Soothing and healing.

Tremolite- For stuck habitual patterns and learning difficulties. Excellent essence to ease training stress.

Tunnelite- Indicated for indoor animals. Helps to reestablish communion with nature and all life forms. Brings peace and wholeness.

Turquoise- Supreme essence for indoor animals, as it deepens the connection to the Soul of the Earth. Cleanses and attunes the energy fields to the sacredness of all life. Provides psychic protection from environmental toxicity.

Ulexite- Balances the chakras. Eases exposure to electromagnetic pollution in computers, electrical power stations and power lines.

Vauxite- Excellent to use with sound and light healing.

Villaumite- Eases difficulty from chemical ingestion (sodium fluoride) in drinking water from city water systems.

Willemite- Good group harmony essence. Promotes loving expression through recognition of common bond.

Woodwardite- Excellent for the elimination of toxic substances from the body, particularly from environmental pollutants.

Xonotlite- Good for healing crises. Strengthens the energy field. Provides the awareness of deeper love.

Zincite- Grounding. Balances lower chakras. Balances energies between pineal gland and the thyroid and adrenal systems.

Starlight Elixirs

"Starlight elixirs are the front runners of vibrational healing modalities for the new millennium. They resonate the frequency of consciousness that all species of Earth are moving toward in this next age."

One of the newest and most exciting energetic remedies being created, starlight elixirs bring even greater dimension to the world of vibrational remedies. Captured from stars, planets and suns from galaxies near and far, these energies are present to assist all beings who live on planet Earth.

Starlight elixirs are captured in the pristine high mountains, far from people, noise, light and power pollution. Using a high-powered telescope with silver-coated mirrors, the telescope tracks the star as it moves through the heavens with a clock-drive device. The energy of the star is captured in a quartz bottle filled with pure water, which is suspended in front of the eyepiece. Inert gas devices are also used to eliminate any possible thought-form contamination. After a two-hour process, this mother solution is preserved with pure grain alcohol. According to the developers of the starlight elixirs, the most amazing aspect of this process is witnessing the design that is revealed in the water of the quartz bottle. The actual pattern of the star dances in the water.

Many planets, stars and suns are much older than the Earth, and the energies captured from these worlds are ancient as well. This information and assistance comes from the beings and civilizations that dwell there and are in support of all life on our planet. Though this may seem outrageous to some, it is becoming increasingly obvious that there *must* be other lifeforms present in the heavens, throughout this Universe of countless billions of worlds. The support is unique to each star, and covers the gamut in scope and character. From accelerating the DNA to assistance in assimilation of minerals and the balance of all aspects of being, starlights are an important support team only recently being discovered. In combination with flowers, gems and elements, they can bring wisdom and assistance from the highest planes into the densest earthly patterns.

Available through Pegasus Products, Inc. in Colorado, there are currently nearly 200 starlight elixirs available, and more on the way. With current research and data still in the early stages, the stars listed in the "Starlight Elixir Qualities" chapter are specifically suited for animals. Perhaps future research with the other starlights continuing to be available will reveal several more especially for our animal friends.

The high frequency of cosmic energy and information that comes through the starlight elixirs can be immediately felt. The extra care required in the handling and administration of these essences is important, as they are light sensitive and cannot be exposed to direct sunlight for long. They are sold in non-toxic, hand painted light-proof bottles to protect the delicate frequencies. I find it best to open them in dim or candle light, and administer them directly on the animal's body or by mouth (slightly diluted).

Obviously, animals haven't the fixed belief systems, negative thought-forms or limited consciousness that many human beings do with regard to unorthodox systems of healing. With an open mind, watch the results that can come, even immediately, with the loving union of energies between animal species and the species of other worlds.

Starlight Elixir Qualities

*"How hard to realize that every camp of men or beast
has this glorious starry firmament for a roof!
In such places standing alone on the mountaintop
it is easy to realize that whatever special nests we make—
leaves and moss like the marmots and birds, or tents or piled stone—
we all dwell in a house of one room—the world with a firmament for
its roof—and are sailing the celestial spaces without leaving any track."*
—John Muir

Adhara- Enhances the absorption of minerals in food.

Aldebaran- Provides peaceful, loving assistance during loss and grief.

Alkaid- Assists animals with a more vegetarian diet, lessens predator/hunter drive.

Alludra- Awakens and strengthens the physical body. Combines well with gold gem elixir.

Alphard- Transmutes anger to love. Good for horses.

Alpheratz- Indicated for leukemia and nerve damage. Regenerating, particularly of the nerves and nervous system. Excellent cell regenerator, especially after a long, chronic illness. Combine with xenon inert gas for even more regenerative affect.

Arneb- Cleanses arterial obstruction, heart disease, and circulatory obstruction in the upper body.

Asellus Borealis- Enhances the heart center, energetically and physically.

Betelgeuse- Transmutes survival and fight or flight instinct to higher centers. Excellent for trauma recovery. Relieves deep fears.

Cheleb- Promotes intimacy through sound and music communication.

Cor Caroli- Assists creatures who live in areas compromised by radiation toxicity, negative geopathic zones, high electrical fields and computer and TV monitors. Excellent when combined with elements and inert gases to aid their absorption.

Dubhe- Assists animals in strengthening their ability to project warming, healing and regenerating energy from the heart to themselves and others.

Enif- Promotes group harmony. Enhances loving communication.

Epsilon Persei- Provides nourishment, with radiance and warmth.

Fomalhaut- Provides assistance in releasing patterns of addictive behavior.

Helios- Excellent for indoor animals. Restores vitality, energy, zest for life. Brings in positive male energy.

Izar- Deeply nurturing. Provides a deeper attunement to life forces and prana. Balancing.

M13- Provides a deeper awareness of love and assistance from the angelic realms.

M44- Promotes surrender and trust in life during times of loss.

M46- Assists group harmony.

M52- Aids creation of conscious community through attunement to dogs, cats, dolphins, and other marine mammals.

M67- Helps animals to open and give love to animals of other species.

Mintaka- Helps animals to better understand their purpose on Earth, and interaction with the human species. Balances aggressive natures.

Mirach- Increases the ability to hear the sounds of the Earth and Mother nature. Enhances healing with nature and sound.

Mirfak- Excellent for cleansing and detoxification at all levels.

Pluto- Assists in breaking down and releasing stuck energies on all levels, including toxins, parasites, bacteria, and viral infection. Works in a deeply subconscious way to bring dark memories and images to the surface for release. Good for healing trauma. Helps in adjusting to change with grace and balance.

Procyon- Increases telepathic communication with other beings. Enhances the ability to absorb energy directly from plants, the Earth and the sun. Excellent for indoor animals.

Rasalhague- Excellent for show animals, particularly dressage horses. Brings beauty, joy and flow in movement.

Sargas- Very good for severely traumatized animals and ferile animals. Strengthens the will to survive.

Saturn Nebula- Strengthens the heart during times of grief and loss.

Scheat- Provides a deeper awareness of interconnection to the Galaxy and all beings.

Schedar- Promotes a spiritual interrelatedness between animals and other animals or people in the environment.

Sirius- Especially for dogs, this essence helps them to understand their purpose and place in the scheme of things, in their home environment and on Earth. Good for cats who have trouble relating to dogs. Assists animals in learning and assimilating information.

***Tarazed*-** Enhances the ability to give and receive love. Gives greater awareness of heart energy. Good combined with gold gem elixir.

***Theta Aurigae*-** Excellent for osteoporosis, arthritis, and the healing of broken bones.

***Vega*-** Provides animals with attunement to their soul vibration, frequency and purpose in themselves, their soul group and their human family.

***Zeta Cygni*-** Supreme remedy for first-aid, trauma and recovery. Assists with all emergencies and crises. Provides immediate relief, though short-lasting. Repeat dosage every two hours.

***Zubenelgenubi*-** Assists in recovery from painful relationships, through release of past trauma. For peaceful relationship.

Elements and Inert Gases

Elements and inert gases are a family of chemical elements, which are chemically inactive and harmless. They do not combine with other elements to form compounds. They are found in the air we breathe, and have been isolated and captured through the technology of inert gas devices. The information for these devices comes through the entity known as Hilarion, and is channeled through Jon Fox, Kevin Ryerson and others.

According to Hilarion, this technology was first used in the mid to late Atlantean period. Developed by Jon Fox and Pegasus Products, the inert gases and elements primarily affect the subtle bodies of living things, as well as the physical body. As of this writing, there are twelve gases and elements that have been developed. They are stabilized in a 16% alcohol and water solution, to be ingested, used topically, or placed in the bath.

The elements provide specific support of all aspects of an animal's being, and work uniquely well with them.

Research information on the affect of these element elixirs on animals is very minimal at this point. The results have been excellent when combined with flower, gem and starlight elixirs. The elements provide amplification, stabilization and new dimension when added to other essences.

Element and Inert Gas Qualities

***Argon*-** Produces energies which are capable of attacking thought-forms that create disease, directly at the etheric level. Excellent in environments where negativity and disease manifest. Good for animals with history of trauma.

***Carbon Dioxide*-** Excellent for animals who are indoors, and do not receive abundant fresh air. Releases excessive carbon dioxide from the body. Aids respiratory difficulties.

***Helium*-** Great stress reliever, especially in the skull. Good for tension. Aids sleep. Anti-viral.

***Hydrogen*-** For animals who are in close attunement to humans and their spiritual process. Excellent for all animals in training, assists releasing old patterns of behavior and learning new ones.

***Krypton*-** Excellent for stimulation of pineal and pituitary glands, especially where light deprivation is a problem. Very good for attacking negative thought-forms in the environment. Provides psychic protection.

***Neon*-** Aids in injury or imbalance to the pelvic bone and spine. Especially healing to the root chakra, and kidney and bladder. Aids well-being. Assists energy field with electromagnetic bombardment from computers and radiation.

***Nitrogen*-** For animals that are indoors and have minimum contact with nature. Provides a greater awareness of plants and nature.

***Oxygen*-** Opens animals to the support of God's love. Good for relationships. Less potent than ozone, but longer lasting effects will be noted.

***Ozone*-** Strengthening, energizing and rejuvenating to all aspects of the body. Cleansing to the electrical body. Opens the connection to Spirit.

***Xenon*-** Excellent for regeneration on all levels, particularly of the tissue. Helps the body to regenerate it's own tissue, mend scars, cuts, burns and broken bones. Aids in the clearing of viral and bacterial organisms. Stimulates pineal and pituitary glands, especially where light deprivation is a problem. Excellent for all abuse, trauma and post-op recovery.

Environmental and Sacred Site Essences

"The living hologram of life radiates the fundamental truth
of the oneness of the whole, and wholeness of the One."

The strength, majesty and beauty of nature are present all around us. In particular, there are focus points on planet Earth of great intensity and profound, sacred beauty. Essence companies are now offering these energies, gathered from various environmental sites and sacred areas, in essence form.

The core support that is offered from environmental essences is very stabilizing, grounding and nurturing. Many of the dramatic climate conditions and pristine environmental locations from which these are gathered could not be experienced otherwise. Even domestic and livestock animals that live in the country are rarely exposed to the wild and the purity of nature found there. For instance, in Alaska, (the Alaskan Flower Essence Project), essences that are captured from the twenty-four hour, twenty-two foot tidal cycle on the edge of the sea cliffs carry keen support and understanding of the great changes of life, the ebb and flow, giving and receiving. Where else could such intensity of understanding and upliftment come from nature?

Environmental essence developers such as Steve Johnson (Alaskan Flower Essence Project) and Sharon Callahan (Anaflora), work in intimate concert with nature to discover, research, develop and capture these unique support systems. Sacred sites, from the Chalice Well in Glastonbury, England, or the rock waters from the sacred fairy wells, carry angelic assistance and attunement to the clearest, most loving aspects of Mother God and nature. For animals who need this supportive attunement, whether in trauma, post-op recovery, a lethargic slump or chronically indoors, these sacred and environmental remedies can work wonders. All animals that remain caged or suffer from kennel stress will benefit greatly from them.

As potent as environmental and sacred site essences are, a very little bit goes a long way. For them to work especially well, when administering, invite the devic elemental forces and overlighting spirits of nature to be present in the healing.

Environmental and Sacred Site Essence Qualities

Blue Springs Rock Water (Anaflora) - Wonderful revitalizing and renewing essence for any creature that lacks enthusiasm and zest for life. Fosters attunement to nature spirits. Excellent for seniors of all species.

Chalice Well (Alaska) - Excellent for trauma, abuse and post-op recovery. Helps to open animals to the support of angels and nature.

Full Moon Reflection (Alaska) - Assists animals in lifting deep, unresolved issues for awareness and healing.

Glacier River (Alaska) - Excellent for animals who have stuck patterns of behavior. Aids resistance to change and all training regimens.

Greenland Ice Cap (Alaska) - Cleanses old and toxic energies from all aspects of being. An excellent training essence, aiding animals in releasing resistance to change.

Liard Hot Springs (Alaska) - Helps restore innocence. Revives body and spirit. Excellent for trauma recovery.

Northern Lights (Alaska) - Deeply transformative heart healer. Excellent for trauma recovery.

Panther Spring Rock Water (Anaflora) - Facilitates telepathic communication between animals and humans, especially when taken by both. Helps humans to understand the animal's purpose for being in their lives. Sparks joy and spontaneity.

Polar Ice (Alaska) - Provides patience during transition.

Portage Glacier (Alaska) - Purifies all bodies from toxic energy.

Rainbow Glacier (Alaska) - For disassociation. Helps to ground.

Solstice Storm (Alaska) - Excellent for purification of the immediate environment and electrical system of all beings.

Solstice Sun (Alaska) - Increases the ability to receive energy from the sun. Excellent for indoor animals.

Squaw Spring Rock Water (Anaflora) - Renews connection to angels. Wonderful for animals who are burdened, stressed and overwhelmed, especially service and therapy animals. Provides nurturing.

Tidal Forces (Alaska) - Supreme remedy for understanding and release of grief. Calms emotional agitation that animals can experience during transition and loss. Helps to accept flow and tides of life with safety and trust. Supports release.

Essences Are for People, Too

"Transformation of the world begins with transformation of oneself at the level of one's own heart."
—Alex Grey

Though the vibrational remedies in this book are specific to animal healing and support, they can also be used for people with similar affect. Many of the remedies available enhance people's attunement to nature and the animal realm.

Before initiating a healing regimen for your animal with energetic remedies, it can be excellent for you to experience them first. This can enhance their effectiveness with your animals. The very best way to understand them is to use them, and give them to your animals. Learning about their qualities is recommended, but remember, there is so much more that these tinctures do than any of us yet know. There is no substitute for experience. Let the essences teach you directly!

Essences to Assist People to Attune to Animals and Nature

FLOWERS

Bear Grass- Excellent for attuning to the world of animals.

Bird of Paradise- Increases understanding of birds, particularly wild. Good for people who work in aviaries, bird breeders and handlers. Territoriality, flight, and movement are better understood.

Bog Rosemary- Helps humans (particularly children) release fear of animals.

Borage- Encourages heart bonding with one's animals.

Calendula- Strengthens ties between people and animals and people and nature.

Chinese Wisteria- Excellent for practitioners who are sensitive to animal's subtle bodies. This will enhance therapy, particularly if the animal takes it too.

Coffee- Helps aquatic animals to commune with humans and vice versa

Cosmos- Excellent for communion and communication, particularly with horses.

Curry Leaf Tree- Promotes group harmony, especially between animals and humans.

Daffodil- Aids in attuning to animals and other living creatures, particularly telepathically.

Delphinium- Very good essence for animal caregivers and practitioners. Enhances telepathic communication with animals as well as the devic realms.

Gentian- For deeper interspecies communication.

Grapefruit- Promotes telepathy between dolphins and humans.

Hyssop- Excellent remedy for forgiveness of any harm that we as humans have caused to animals. Helps to release shame and promote clarity

118

between species. For seeing the highest soul purpose of the animal realm.

Jade Vine- Promotes heart-centered communication, particularly between animals and people.

Monkshood- Helps humans release fear of animals.

Noble Star Flower Cactus- Brings a blending of love energies and a conscious awareness of the consequences of eating meat. Assists those who wish, to transition to a vegetarian diet. Promotes in humans the willingness to assist the animals of this world.

O'hia Lehua- Assists attunement to thought-forms of plants and animals. Stimulates inner animal nature of people at the highest level.

Partridgeberry- Enhances relationships between animals and humans.

Perilla- Increases the healing energy that pours from the hands. Excellent for people who work with animals, especially those who use hands-on healing techniques of any kind.

Shrimp Plant- Provides greater awareness of the angelic nature of whales, dolphins, and other sea creatures.

Soapberry- Helps humans release their fear of animals.

GEMS

Agate (Moss)- Excellent essence to assist people to attune to nature.

Andradite- Facilitates attunement to dolphins and their energy.

Arthurite- Promotes in people a deeper love of animals, plants and the Earth.

Astrophyllite- Enhances telepathic communication with other beings.

Beaudantite- Attunes people to the common thread of love between all creatures.

Brochantite- Brings clearer awareness in people of the etheric bodies of plants and animals.

Coral (Red/White)- Assists people to attune to animals and nature.

Emerald- Universal heart cleanser and balancer. Excellent for staying emotionally clear and connected to your animal. Very helpful for loss and grief.

Hancockite- Promotes a deeper understanding of animals.

Larimar- Helps people to attune to the energies of dolphins and whales.

Lirconite- Assists people in healing work with animals.

Papagoite- Aids people in animal communion.

Rhodocrocite- For humans who have difficulty relating and bonding with animals and nature, especially due to past trauma and emotional pain. Restores equilibrium in heart and body.

Turquoise- Attunes and connects the energy field to the oneness and sacredness of the Earth and all life.

STARS

Adhara- Assists in shifting the vibratory rate of the bodies of human beings, to experience oneness with animals.

Asellus Australis- Aids in communication with animals, particularly mammals that are wild. Promotes trust in communication. Good to take with the animal.

Cheleb- Promotes intimacy through high levels of communication. Assists in sound healing. Increases the ability to give and receive, cutting through barriers of wounds and past relationship difficulty.

Dubhe- Strengthens the ability to project warming, healing, and regenerating energy from the heart, which can be directed with greater consciousness to animals (or any species).

Enif- Enhances unity and harmony in small groups, encouraging loving communication and group attunement.

M44- For people who are experiencing the loss of their pet. Assists with release and understanding. Aids in the surrender and trust of life.

M47- Promotes reverence for life and the ability to work with the devic realm.

M52- For individuals who wish for a deeper understanding and awareness of humanity's relationship to primates. Promotes deeper interaction with animals, particularly primates, dolphins, and cats.

M67- Assists people who work with vibrational medicines and especially essences, in understanding the underlying principles and very nature of the Universe. Helps one to connect with the purpose of all life.

Merope- Helps one to understand the ability to communicate with the animal realm.

Scheat- Promotes deeper awareness of our interconnection to the Galaxy, and other beings.

Schedar- Promotes a deeper awareness of the spiritual interrelationship between the realms of nature: the plants, the animals and the Earth.

Sirius- Gives supreme assistance in understanding and creating a working knowledge of the purpose and nature of dogs on Earth.

Tarazed- Provides greater ability to give and receive love. Allows greater expansion of heart energy, especially when combined with gold gem elixir.

Vega- Allows deeper attunement to oneselves and one's animal's soul frequency and purpose, individually and together.

Zeta Cygni- Excellent first-aid remedy during times of emergency, trauma or stress, especially when it is necessary to be calm and provide care.

Zubenelgenubi- Especially beneficial for painful relationships. Allows all parties to release past trauma and aggression that has caused friction in the past. Allows for peaceful relationship.

INERT GAS ELIXIRS

Carbon Dioxide- Creates a powerful bridge between human and plant families.

Hydrogen- Promotes understanding of the fundamental oneness behind God and all life forms.

Neon- Promotes a deeper connection to the Earth.

Nitrogen- Encourages greater awareness of plants.

ENVIRONMENTAL AND SACRED SITES

Chalice Well- Attunes people to the awareness of support constantly available from the angelic, elemental and plant realms. Strengthens the connection with the Earth.

Panther Spring Rock Water- Facilitates telepathic communication between animals and humans, especially when taken together. Helps people to understand the animal's purpose for being in their lives. Promotes joy and spontaneity.

Special Combinations

Combining various types of vibrational remedies (flower, gem, starlight, etc.) can create powerful infused tinctures that are just beginning to be explored. When these are combined with pure essential oils, the energetic hologram is even more effective. Though very little research has been done in combining the aromas and vibrational remedies, my experience in using them together has been profound. They catalyze the energetic properties in each other, and their effect, particularly when used as a spray, is remarkable and immediate. My sensing is that a multi-dimensional hologram is created and conveyed through the blend itself. It is also my experience that the starlight elixirs become stable in light when in combination with other types of vibrational remedies, especially when essential oils are used, and the oils also act as preservative for the entire combination.

Several essence companies throughout the world have prepared excellent vibrational remedy combinations specifically for animal health and healing, though most of these companies are not as yet combining essences with aromatherapy oils. Listed below are some of these companies, and the combinations which they offer, along with brief descriptions.

ALASKAN FLOWER ESSENCE PROJECT

Soul Support (formerly Emergency Care) - Brings strength and stability during emergencies, stress, trauma and transformation.

Travel Ease- Specifically designed to ease the negative effects of air travel, including what is commonly referred to as jet lag.

Fireweed Combo- Supports the processes of transformation, transition, and change.

Sacred Space Formula- Creates and maintains a clear and vibrant energy field in the home or office.

Purification Formula- Breaks up and cleanses stagnant patterns of energy on any level.

Guardian Formula- An invocation formula that helps create a powerful forcefield of protection in the aura.

Calling All Angels- An invocation formula that helps to contact the love, guidance, and protection of the angelic realm.

ALOHA FLOWER ESSENCES

Acceptance- Acceptance of disability and old age.

Adjustment- Adjustment to new family or environment.

Aftershock- Post-operative, accident or trauma.

Fear- Of animals, people or environment.

Separation- Eases pain from separation from loved ones.

ANAFLORA

Aggression- Calming and soothing, especially for dogs and horses.

Bereavement- Gives comfort in the loss of an animal's loved one. For animals and people.

Calm Kitty- Eases stress and nervousness. For people too!

Captivity- Lessens the shock of captivity to wild animals.

Christ Consciousness- Opens people and animals to this high frequency.

Essence of Nature- For cats who are strictly indoors and light and nature deprived.

Expanded States- Enables animals to experience ecstatic states with their humans.

Feral Cat Comforter- Calming and nurturing for the undomesticated cat.

Freedom- Aids animals who are to be released into the wild.

Fur and Feather- For harmony between cats and birds, indoor and out.

Good Dog!- Aids in training of any kind. Helps focus, and relieves resistance.

Harmony- To aid animals when a new member (animal or human) arrives.

Loneliness- For animals who spend much of their time alone.

Pound Puppies, and Kittens Too!- Eases all aspects of kennel stress. Promotes love and trust.

Recovery Remedy- General-purpose trauma remedy for people and animals.

Relocation- For both people and animals, when moving to a new location.

Return to Joy- For abuse victims. Builds trust and opens the heart.

Senior Formula- Aids all difficulty associated with aging (physical, mental and emotional).

Service Animals- For all animals who "work for a living". Eases the overburdened heart.

Spay and Neuter- Restores energy balance after these procedures.

Special Stress- Especially for animals who are exposed to human stress.

St. Francis Formula for Injured Wild Birds- Excellent for trauma.

Telepathy- To be taken by animals and people together. Increases spiritual communication and communion.

Transition- Eases discomfort and fear in preparing for death.

Tranquility- Calming and soothing. Especially for animals that are hyperactive.

DESERT ALCHEMY

Cellular Joy Formula- For releasing fear and trauma from physical abuse. Restores trust in humans and human touch.

Clearing and Releasing Formula- Cleanses toxic energy from animal's energy field. Provides protection.

Community Spirit Formula- Good group harmony essence. Supports healthy boundaries.

Crisis Desert Energy Formula- Excellent to assist animals in staying centered during crisis of any kind.

Embracing Humanness Formula- Good for animals who are learning to live with humans, especially wild and sanctuaried animals.

Emotional Awareness Formula- Allows animals to safely feel, or to level out emotionally. Emotionally balancing.

Experiencing Your Feeling Formula- Allows animals to access joy, especially in difficult emotional situations.

Five Elements Formula- A combination for each element, created to balance each element within each individual.

Immune Formula- Assists in keeping an internal balance, healthy boundaries and strong will connected to Source.

New Mother's Formula- Aids the mothering instinct. Provides nurturance for mom and infant.

Transition Formula- Provides stability and peace during change and transition into new surroundings or death.

Unconditional Love and Support Formula- Opens the channel in animals to receive and give unconditional love, especially after trauma or abuse.

Wind & Storm Formula- Assists animals to flow and remain centered during times of chaos and upheaval.

FLOWER ESSENCE SOCIETY

Five Flower Formula- For shock, trauma, acute and post-op stress, as well as abuse. Aids in transport, and helps with taking in food or water during times of stress.

GREEN HOPE FARM

Animal Emergency Care- For trauma, shock and acute stress in any emergency condition.
Flea Free- For alleviation of any parasitic condition, physical or vibrational.
Healthy Coat- Good for fur and coats of animals.
Restore- Cleanses the physical and energetic bodies while it balances and centers.
Show Cats- Provides emotional balance for cats and over-sensitive animals who display shyness or hostility.
Watch Your Back- Keeps the energy moving through the spine and spinal chakras. Particularly for horses.

PEGASUS PRODUCTS

Pegasus has an extensive line of combinations. Contact them directly (see Resources) for complete information.

Animal Combinations:

New Patterns- Assistance with major shifts and transitions.
Graceful Aging- Physical support during the aging process.
Flexibility- Aids physical, emotional and mental flexibility.
Fertility- For both males and females.
Birthing- For pre-natal and birthing.
Spay/Neuter- Provides support for these procedures.
Post-Op- Provides emotional and physical support after surgery. Helps detox drug residue.
Vitality- Provides energy, cheerfulness and liveliness.
Stress-Free- Provides deep relaxation.
New Diet- For assistance in vegetarian, raw or healthier diet transition.
Boundaries- Assists animals when moving to a new space, or when others (animal and human) move into theirs.
Performer- Provides support for performers as well as an increase in athletic ability.
Athlete- Provides support and increases agility and endurance.
Communication- Assists in communication between species.
Learning- Assists in all training.
Bones/Joints- For all difficulties with bones and soft tissue.
Sleep- Assists all sleep difficulties.
Travel- For relocation and travel by car, plane, etc.
Weight Gain- Assists the metabolism and body in gaining weight.
Weight Loss- Especially good for animals after weight gain from pregnancy, or older, neutered and spayed animals.

Pests- Assists in clearing fleas, flies, etc. Provides emotional support.

1st Aid- Excellent for all trauma. For internal and external use.

Abandonment- Provides emotional assistance for the trauma of abandonment.

Jealousy- Helps with sharing space and energy.

Self-Esteem- Provides core support.

Shyness- Helps with fear of humans and other animals.

Aggression- Eases and calms aggressive behaviors.

Mouth/Jaw- For all difficulties related to this area, physical and emotional. Excellent for barking and biting.

Hearing- Aids in hearing issues.

Sense of Smell- Aids in problems with sense of smell.

Sense of Touch- Increases physical sensitivity.

Sight- Aids vision difficulties.

Hair, Skin and Nails- For regeneration, includes claws, feathers, beaks, scales and fur!

Other Combinations:

A Dozen Roses- Provides the support of the highest octave of love from the most highly evolved flower species: the roses. Gives supreme divine and loving support from twelve of the most beautiful roses.

Aetheric Waterfall- Very cleansing for the energetic bodies, especially after surgical procedures or drugs of any kind.

Angels- For angelic support when needed. Excellent for indoor and light deprived animals.

Animal Attunement- To assist people and animals to attune to other animals.

Aura Spray- Cleanses and lifts all dense energies in the animal's energetic field as well as the environment. Good used with massage.

Corals- Balances chakras. Excellent for circulation, heart function and bones.

Diamond- Clears and balances all bodies. Powerful energizer and balancer. Enhances other remedies.

Earth Healing- Profoundly deepens the connection to the Earth. Especially good for animals who are indoors and light deprived.

Grounding- Excellent for healing crisis, emotional or physical imbalance of any kind. Excellent for aid in surgery recovery, in travel, when your animal is "out of sorts" for any reason.

Joy- Provides joy, Joy, JOY!

One Heart- Opens the heart to give and receive love. Promotes deeper and more loving relationships.

Pregnancy- Excellent remedy for pregnancy and post-partum. Energetically tones female organs.

Protection- Puts a vibratory shield in place. Provides protection from negative influence of all kinds in the environment. Excellent for animals who are highly sensitive.

Sapphire- Wonderfully energizing and balancing to the chakras.

Vegetarianism- To aid animals who eat other animals, to lessen the predator instinct.

Yarrows- Excellent for defense against negativity and radiation. Protects all chakras in a shield of light.

Vibrational Remedies Cross-Reference

Abandonment/Neglect

F- Evening Primrose, Evening Star, Forget-Me-Not, Foxglove, Maltese Cross, Mariposa Lily, Oak, Pleurisy Root, Queen of the Night, Red Clover, Single Delight, Woven Spine Pineapple Cactus, Yellow Dryas.

G- Amethyst, Datolite, Diamond-Pink, Sapphire, Sarabauite.

S- M13, M44, Zeta Cygni.

E- Oxygen, Ozone.

Abuse/Trauma

F- Agave, Arnica, Balsam Poplar, Bamboo Orchid, Barley, Birch, Black Currant, Black-Eyed Susan, Bo Tree, Bottlebrush, California Wild Rose, Cat's Ears (Star Tulip), Cinnamon, Clarkia, Clematis, Columbine, Comfrey, Coral Root, Corn, Cottongrass, Cottonwood, Dandelion, Dracaena, Dwarf Fireweed, Easter Lily, Ephedra, Evening Primrose, Evening Star, Feverfew, Fireweed, Goldenrod, Goldenseal, Grape Hyacinth, Grass of Parnassus, Hooded Ladies Tresses, Horsetail, Inmortal, Kamani, Labrador Tea, Ladies Tresses, Lobelia, Lotus, Love Lies Bleeding, Lungwort, Maltese Cross, Mariposa Lily, Meadowsweet, Mesquite, Milkweed, Monkshood, Mushroom, Northern Ladies Slipper, Oak, Ocotillo, Old Maid, Olive, Onion, Orange Flame Flower Cactus, Pansy, Pennyroyal, Penstemon, Pine, Pink Monkeyflower, Plantain, Pleurisy Root, Pomegranate, Queen Anne's Lace, Queen of the Night, Red Bud, River Beauty, Rosa Hardii, Rosa Macrophylla, Rosa Nutkana, St. John's Wort, Sacred Datura, Saguaro, Scarlet Runner Bean, Self-Heal, Star of Bethlehem, Strawberry, Sweet Briar, Sweet Pea, Sweetgrass, Thurber's Gilia, Tundra Twayblade,

128

Uala, White Fireweed, Wild Sweet Pea, Woven Spine Pineapple Cactus, Yarrow, Yerba Santa, Yucca.
G- Aquamarine, Barite, Brucite, Chrysocolla, Coral-Black, Diamond-Pink, Emerald, Epistilbite, Garnet-Rhodolite, Jasper-Green, Opal, Quartz-Rose, Sapphire, Sarabauite, Star Sapphire, Tiger's Eye, Topaz.
S- Betelgeuse, Sargas, Zeta Cygni, Zubenelgenubi.
E- Argon, Carbon Dioxide, Oxygen, Ozone, Xenon.
SS- Chalice Well, Liard Hot Springs, Northern Lights.

Aggression/Anger

F- Almond, Alyssum, Antimony, Apple, Apricot, Aspen, Avocado, Barley, Beech, Bo Tree, Cedar, Compass Barrel Cactus, Elm, Eucalyptus, Feverfew, Fireweed, Fuchsia, Garlic, Grapefruit, Holly, Jerusalem Artichoke, Kidney Bean, Nectarine, Oak, Ocotillo, Orange Flame Flower Cactus, Oregon Grape Root, Peach, Pear, Pine, Pleurisy Root, Rattlesnake Plantain Orchid, Redwood, Snapdragon, Spruce, Tiger Lily, Uala, Walnut, Ylang Ylang, Yucca.
G- Barite, Cassiterite, Chrysoprase, Epistilbite, Lazulite, Ruby, Sarandite, Tiger's Eye.
S- Adhara, Alphard, Mintaka.
E- Carbon Dioxide.

Aging

F- Blackberry, Borage, Cerato, Mallow, Tree Opuntia.
G- Copper, Coral-Red.
E- Oxygen, Ozone, Xenon.
SS- Blue Springs Rock Water.

Allergies

F- Beech, Cedar, Crab Apple, Screw Pine, Willow.

Aloofness/Alienation/Withdrawal/Shyness

F- Amaranthus, Avocado, Chaparral, Evening Star, Frangipani, French Marigold, Hedgehog Cactus, Jojoba, Manzanita, Mariposa Lily, Mezereum, Mesquite, Milkmaids, Mimulus, Nectarine, Queen of the Night, Sensitive Plant, Shooting Star, Snapdragon, Star Tulip, Tundra Twayblade, Water Violet.
G- Garnet-Rhodolite.
S- Betelgeuse, Cheleb.
E- Neon, Oxygen, Ozone.
SS- Rainbow Glacier.

Anemia

F- Chestnut Bud, Gentian, Mesquite, Olive, Star of Bethlehem, Walnut.
G- Manganese.
E- Neon, Oxygen, Ozone, Xenon.

Antibiotics & Drugs (removal)

F- Cedar, Coral Root (Spotted), Garlic, Pine Drops.
E- Oxygen, Ozone.

Anxiety

F- Agrimony, Aspen, Basil, Borage, Chamomile, Chrysanthemum, Clove, Cosmos, Dandelion, Dill, Figwort, Frangipani, Fuschia, Garlic, Impatiens, Jacob's Ladder, Jumping Cholla Cactus, Kohlrabi, Licorice, Loquat, Mallow, Milkmaids, Mimulus, Mugwort, Mushroom, Passion Flower, Pleurisy Root, Poison Ivy, Potato, Rabbitbrush, Star Tulip, Sweet Flag, White Chestnut.
G- Azurite/Malachite, Carletonite, Jadeite, Jet, Quartz-White, Sardonyx.
E- Carbon Dioxide, Neon.
SS- Tidal Forces.

Appetite (lack of)

F- Manzanita, Paw Paw.
E- Neon.

Aromatherapy (enhancement)

F- Ginger, Jasmine, Jojoba, Sandalwood, Tuberose.
G- Cobaltite.

Arthritis

G- Azurite.
S- Theta Aurigae.
E- Oxygen, Ozone, Xenon.

Assimilation of Nutrients

F- Paw Paw, Vitex.
G- Agate-Moss, Chromium, Cobaltian Calcite.
S- Adhara.
E- Carbon Dioxide.

Balance (energetic)

F- Aconite, Alyssum, Amaranthus, Barley, Buffalo Gourd, California Bay Laurel, California Pitcher Plant, Fairy Duster, Golden Seal, Grass of Parnassus, Indian Pipe, Lotus, Orchid, Parsley, Pineapple, Sacred Datura, Star of Bethlehem, Wisteria.
G- Anapoite, Okenite, Opal, Ruby, Silver, Ulexite, Xonotlite, Zincite.
S- Pluto.
E- Oxygen, Ozone.
SS- Tidal Forces.

Balance (emotional)

F- Allamanda, Bear Grass, Buffalo Gourd, California Poppy, Cape Honeysuckle, Cat's Tail, Cinnamon, Clematis, Dandelion, Elecampagne, Fennel, Geranium, Ginko Biloba, Hawthorne, Hedgehog Cactus, Jerusalem Artichoke, Jumping Cholla Cactus, Labrador Tea, Larkspur, Lobelia, Lotus, Macadamia, Monkeyflower Bush, Pecan.
G- Callaghanite, Chrysoprase, Emerald, Lepidolite, Moonstone, Opal, Quartz-White, Ruby, Sodalite, Topaz.
S- Mintaka, Pluto.

Balance (physical)

F- California Bay Laurel, Cotton Grass, Dandelion, Fairy Duster, Goldenseal, Heliconia, Jasmine, Melon Loco, Orchid, Wood Betony, Ylang Ylang.
G- Diamond-White, Ruby.
S- Pluto.
E- Neon.

Barking

F- Banana, Cerato, Chamomile, Chestnut Bud, Heather, Vervain.
G- Aquamarine, Beryl, Lapis Lazuli, Tourmaline-Blue, Turquoise.

Behavior Patterns (stubborn)

F- Agrimony, Alyssum, Blackberry, Black Spruce, California Poppy, Cayenne, Chestnut Bud, Cosmos, Dandelion, Goldenseal, Grass of Parnassus, Hairy Butterwort, Holly, Labrador Tea, Macadamia, Morning Glory, Orange, Pine, Plantain, Round Leaved Sundew, Sunflower, Walnut, Whitethorn, White Chestnut, White Fireweed.
G- Azurite/Malachite, Duftite, Herderite.
S- Fomalhaut, Pluto.

131

E- Hydrogen.
SS- Glacier River.

Birds

F- Bird of Paradise, Bo, Bottlebrush, Dandelion, Foxglove, French Marigold, Gilia (Scarlet), Wild Oat (pulling out feathers).

Birth

F- Almond, Alyssum, Balm of Gilead, Chervil, Coconut, Crocus, Evening Primrose, Green Bells of Ireland, Grove Sandwort, Magnolia, Mala Mujer, Noni, Pineapple Weed, Pomegranate, Spirea, Squash.
G- Moonstone.
E- Carbon Dioxide, Helium, Neon, Nitrogen, Oxygen, Ozone, Xenon.

Birth First-Aid

F- Dracaena, Mala Mujer, Northern Ladies Slipper, Onion, Shooting Star, Walnut.
G- Chalcedony, Coral-Black, Sapphire.
S- Zeta Cygni.
E- Neon, Oxygen, Ozone, Xenon.

Bladder

F- Evening Primrose, Irish Moss, Sea Lettuce, Swamp Onion.

Bleeding

F- Agrimony, Elm.
S- Zeta Cygni.

Blockages

F- Bells of Ireland, Calliandra, Macadamia, Rosa Macrantha, Woven Spine Pineapple Cactus.
G- Callaghanite, Coral-Black, Fluorite, Glaucocerinite.
S- Pluto.
E- Argon, Helium.
SS- Chalice Well, Full Moon Reflection, Glacier River, Greenland Icecap.

Blood

F- Bloodroot, Pink Laurel.
G- Aegerine, Berthierite, Bloodstone, Hematite, Jade.
E- Neon.

Body/Soul Fusion

Strengthening (of physical body)
F- Allamanda, Apricot, Calendula, Cedar, Coconut, Comfrey, Cotton, Elephant's Head, Fennel, Jojoba, Lotus, Mallow, Papaya, Sunflower, Wisteria.
G- Aventurine, Brass, Brucite, Gold, Kutnahorite, Okenite.
S- Alludra, Izar, Pluto.

Fusing
F- Arnica, Dutch Broom, Fireweed, Monkshood, Northern Ladies Slipper, Olive, Pink Laurel, Yellow Dryas.
G- Azurite/Malachite, Beryl, Dumortierite, Garnet-Rhodolite, Malachite, Szenicsite.
S- Sargas, Schedar, Sirius, Vega.

Stabilizing
F- Bougainvillea, Ephedra, Ginger, Goldenrod, Gum Plant, Jimson Weed, Lavender, Lima Bean, Nutmeg, Pennyroyal, Red Rugosa Rose, Vitex, Yucca.
G- Herkimer Diamond, Jet, Krupkaite, Moldavite, Philipsburgite, Quartz-Brazilian, Rhodocrocite, Spectrolite, Turquoise, Woodwardite.
E- Nitrogen.
SS- Tidal Forces.

Bones

F- Banana, Borage, Comfrey.
G- Calcite, Coral-Black, Coral-Red, Sandstone, Sulfur.
S- Sirius, Theta Aurigae.
E- Xenon.

Boundaries

F- Calothalmus Validas, Canyon Grapevine, Cedar, Chaulmoogra Hydnocarpus, Desert Barrel Cactus, Hop Tree, Hyssop, Lion's Tail, Mountain Pennyroyal, One-Sided Wintergreen, St. John's Wort, Tansy, Thistle, Wintergreen, Wormwood, Yarrow.
G- Covellite.

Bronchitis

F- Blackberry, Eucalyptus, Holly, Jasmine, Lobelia.
E- Carbon Dioxide, Oxygen, Ozone.

Burns

F- Aconite, Agave, Apple, Arnica, Black-Eyed Susan, California Wild Rose, Clematis, Comfrey, Cotton, Cotton Grass, Dwarf Fireweed, Ephedra, Fireweed, French Marigold, Grass of Parnassus, Hooded Ladies Tresses, Labrador Tea, Lotus, Maltese Cross, Mariposa Lily, Mesquite, Noni, Northern Ladies Slipper, Onion, Orange Flame Flower Cactus, Penstemon, Peony, Pink Monkeyflower, Purple Nightshade, River Beauty, Rock Rose, Rosa Gallica Officinalis, Rosa Macrophylla, Sage, Saguaro, Self-Heal, Sitka Burnett, Star of Bethlehem, Sweet Briar, Sweetgrass, Sweet Chestnut, Tundra Twayblade, Uala, Woven Spine Pineapple Cactus, Yerba Santa, Zinnia, Zucchini.
S- Zeta Cygni.
E- Helium, Oxygen, Ozone, Xenon.
SS- Chalice Well, Northern Lights, Portage Glacier, Squaw Spring Rock Water.

Cage Stress (kennel, vet, and pound stays and confined travel)

F- Aloe Eru, Bottlebrush, Dandelion, Freesia, Luffa, Milo, Quaking Grass, Yerba Santa.
G- Cuproskowdilite, Brucite, Calcite-Orange, Chrysoprase, Clay, Clinoptilolite, Coral-Black, Diamond-Pink, Diamond-White, Garnet-Rhodolite, Gold, Hematite, Herkimer Diamond, Jadeite, Jasper-Green, Jet, Kutnahorite, Malachite, Moonstone, Quartz-Brazilian, Ruby, Silver, Star Sapphire, Topaz, Tourmaline-Black, Turquoise, Villaumite, Zincite.
S- Betelgeuse, Helios, Izar, Mirfak, Pluto, Sargas, Zeta Cygni, Zubenelgenubi.
E- Argon, Carbon Dioxide, Helium, Krypton, Neon, Oxygen, Ozone, Xenon.
SS- Blue Springs Rock Water, Chalice Well, Liard Hot Springs, Northern Lights, Portage Glacier, Rainbow Glacier, Solstice Storm, Solstice Sun, Squaw Spring Rock Water.

Calming

F- Candlenut Tree, Candy Barrel Cactus, Cantaloupe, Chrysanthemum, Cinnamon, Clematis, Clove Tree, Dandelion, Lettuce, Licorice, Mallow, Ocotillo, Self Heal.
G- Jadeite.
S- Mirfak.
E- Oxygen, Ozone.

Cancer

F- Aloe Ciliaris, Apricot, Bleeding Heart, Chaulmoogra Hydnocarpus, Cosmos, Hyssop, Redwood, Spiderwort, Spruce, Sunflower.
G- Abalone, Azurite/Malachite, Clay, Diamond-Pink, Fluorite, Gold, Moonstone, Tourmaline-Blue.
E- Argon, Krypton, Oxygen, Ozone, Xenon.
SS- Full Moon Reflection, Greenland Ice Cap, Liard Hot Springs, Portage Glacier, Squaw Springs Rock Water.

Car Sickness

F- Chestnut Bud, Ginger, Kiwi, Mimulus, Scleranthus, Trillium, Walnut, Whitethorn.
G- Moonstone, Quartz-Smoky, Tourmaline-Black.
S- Zeta Cygni.
E- Carbon Dioxide, Neon, Oxygen, Ozone.
SS- Blue Springs Rock Water, Greenland Ice Cap, Portage Glacier, Rainbow Glacier.

Cats

F- Bloodroot, Catnip, Evening Star, Hedgehog Cactus, Hyssop, Madia, Mala Mujer, Manzanita, Mesquite, Pansy, Saguaro, Sensitive Plant, Star of Bethlehem, Sweet Pea, Tiger Lily, Water Violet.
G- Jasper-Picture, Tiger's Eye.
S- M52.

Circulation

F- California Poppy, Chaparral, Garlic, Red Clover, Sugar Beet.
G- Acharandite, Aegerine, Berthierite, Coral, Jade, Kunzite.
S- Arneb.
E- Oxygen, Ozone, Xenon.
SS- Blue Springs Rock Water, Chalice Well, Glacier River, Greenland Ice Cap, Tidal Forces.

Cleansing

F- Acacia, Barley, Calliandra, Cedar, Comfrey, Crab Apple, Desert Barrel Cactus, Dutchman's Breeches, Dwarf Fireweed, Fireweed, Freesia, Grass of Parnassus, Green Fairy Orchid, Jasmine, Lime, Luffa, Monkeytail, Onion, Sacred Datura, Sage, St. John's Wort, Sitka Burnett, Spanish Bayonet, Sunflower, Swamp Onion.

G- Aventurine, Bismuth, Brass, Callaghanite, Chrysolite, Chrysoprase, Diaboleite, Emerald, Fluorite, Lapis Lazuli, Libethenite, Quartz-Brazilian, Quartz-Citrine, Quartz-Rose, Quartz-Smoky, Rhodocrocite, Tourmaline-Black, Turquoise.
S- Arneb.
E- Ozone, Xenon.
SS- Blue Springs Rock Water, Greenland Ice Cap, Portage Glacier, Solstice Storm.

Colds

F- Crab Apple, Hornbeam.
G- Beryl, Carbon Steel, Copper, Gold, Jet, Sulfur.
S- Alpheratz, Epsilon Persei, Izar, Mirfak.
E- Argon, Carbon Dioxide, Helium, Krypton, Neon, Oxygen, Ozone, Xenon.
SS- Blue Springs Rock Water, Greenland Ice Cap, Portage Glacier, Rainbow Glacier, Solstice Storm, Squaw Spring Rock Water.

Color Therapy (enhancement)

F- Bells of Ireland, Lemon, Nasturtium, Spice Bush.
G- Agate-Fire, Alexandrite.

Communication

F- Bells of Ireland, Cassandra, Cosmos, Dogwood, Gentian, Grove Sandwort, Horsetail, Jade Vine, Lemmon's Paintbrush, Lion's Tail, Macadamia, Manzanita, Melaleuca, Mesquite, Motherwort, Peony, Sacred Datura, Teddy Bear Cholla Cactus, Uala, Walnut.
G- Celestite, Datolite, Kinoite, Tourmaline-Blue, Turquoise.
S- Cheleb, Enif, Procyon.
SS- Panther Springs Rock Water.

Conception

F- Blackberry, Cosmos, Fig.

Constipation

F- Chicory, Elm, Scleranthus.
G- Copper, Coral, Emerald, Halite, Jasper-Green.

Convulsions

G- Amethyst & Silver, blended in equal parts.

Depression

F- Agave, Agave Yaquiana, Aloe Vera, Basil, Blackberry, Bog Blueberry, Borage, Chamomile, Chiming Bells, Chrysanthemum, Compass Barrel Cactus, Coyote Mint, Cucumber, Dill, Fennel, Foxglove, Gardenia, Honeysuckle, Hornbeam, Horseradish, Inmortal, Jumping Cholla Cactus, Lobivia Cactus, Mustard, Noble Star Flower Cactus, Peach, Periwinkle, Poke Weed, Prickly Pear Cactus, Red Bud, Rosa Gallica Officinalis, Sacred Datura, Saguaro, Scotch Broom, Sierra Rein Orchid, Sugar Cane, Tree of Life, Waikiki Rainbow Cactus, Wild Oat, Woven Spine Pineapple Cactus, Ylang Ylang, Yucca.

G- Agate-Botswana, Agate-Moss, Alexandrite, Calcite-Orange, Cavanisite, Diamond-Pink, Jet, Platinum, Pyrite, Quartz-White, Sapphire, Sardonyx, Szenicsite.

S- Asellus Borealis, Tarazed.

E- Argon.

SS- Blue Springs Rock Water, Full Moon Reflection, Liard Hot Springs, Northern Lights.

Diarrhea

F- Crab Apple, Rock Rose.

G- Beryl, Magnesium.

Digestion

F- Avocado, Carrot, Chives, Dandelion, Garlic, Gentian, Potato, Radish, Strawberry.

G- Agate, Clay, Copper, Coral, Jasper, Kunzite.

Dogs

F- Coyote Mint, Goldenseal, Inmortal, Olive, Stinging Nettle, Vervain, Water Violet, Yerba Santa.

G- Glaucocerinite, Krupkaite, Moonstone, Platinum.

S- M52, Sirius.

Dolphins

F- Coffee, Cosmos, Grapefruit, Motherwort, Shrimp Plant.

G- Cobaltite.

S- M52.

Ears (hearing)

F- Allamanda, French Marigold.
S- Mirach.

Elephants

F- Apricot, Crab Apple, Pansy, Tagua, Walnut.
E- Xenon.

Elimination, Improper

F- Black Spruce, Morning Glory, Tiger Lily.

Energy System

F- Acacia, Bamboo, Barley, Black-Eyed Susan, Coconut, Comfrey, Dandelion, Freesia, Grass of Parnassus, Lime, Parsley, Sage, Trumpet Vine.
G- Fluorite, Opal, Quartz-Brazilian, Silver, Spectrolite, Turquoise, Xonotlite.
S- Helios, Mirfak.
E- Neon, Ozone, Xenon.
SS- Blue Springs Rock Water, Greenland Ice Cap, Liard Hot Springs, Portage Glacier, Solstice Storm, Solstice Sun.

Epilepsy

F- Angelica, Amaranthus, Dandelion, Easter Lily, Green Rose, Lilac, Lobelia, Macartney Rose, Star Tulip, Yerba Santa.
G- Agate-Picture, Copper, Diamond, Gold, Silver.

Exhaustion/Overwhelm

F- Buffalo Gourd, Cow Parsnip, Elm, Olive, Penstemon, Star Tulip, Sweet Chestnut, Whitethorn, Wolfberry, Woven Spine Pineapple Cactus, Zucchini.
G- Covellite, Hematite, Tourmaline-Black.
S- Alludra, Alpheratz, Cor Caroli, Dubhe, Epsilon Persei, Helios, Izar, Mirfak, Pluto.
E- Carbon Dioxide, Helium, Krypton, Neon, Ozone, Xenon.
SS- Blue Springs Rock Water, Liard Hot Springs, Panther Spring Rock Water, Portage Glacier, Solstice Storm, Squaw Spring Rock Water.

Eyes

F- Avocado, Elm, Loquat, Peach, Redwood, Spruce, Walnut.
G- Jade.

138

Fatigue

F- Dandelion, Horseradish, Potato, Strawberry.
E- Carbon Dioxide.

Fear (general)

F- Agave, Apple, Asparagus, Aspen, Calendula, Catnip, Cedar, Cherry Plum, Cotton, Evening Primrose, Feverfew, Fig, Figwort, Fuschia, Garlic, Irish Moss, Kelp, Kidney Bean, Kiwi, Larch, Loquat, Lotus, Mimulus, Morning Glory, Mugwort, Peanut, Queen of the Night, Rice, Scarlet Runner Bean, Swamp Onion, Sweet Flag, Tiger Lily, Yucca.
G- Antimony, Aquamarine, Aventurine, Barite, Cassiterite, Diaboleite, Glaucocerinite.
S- Asellus Borealis, Betelgeuse, Epsilon Persei, Pluto, Sargas, Tarazed, Zeta Cygni.
E- Argon, Oxygen, Ozone, Xenon.
SS- Chalice Well, Full Moon Reflection, Greenland Icecap, Liard Hot Springs, Portage Glacier, Squaw Spring Rock Water.

of Animals:
F- Bog Rosemary, Harebell, Holly, Monkshood, St. John's Wort, Soapberry.

of Bonding/Intimacy:
F- Avocado, Birch, Onion, Teddy Bear Cholla Cactus.
G- Diamond-Pink.

of Death:
F- Angel's Trumpet, Lily of the Valley, Mallow, Star Tulip.
G- Copper.

of People:
F- Plantain, Queen Anne's Lace, Queen of the Night, St. John's Wort, Yerba Santa, Yucca.

of Transition:
F- Aspen, Loquat, Rhododendron, Sweet Flag, Thurber's Gillia, Yerba Santa.
G- Aventurine.

Feet

F- Ladies Slipper, Lima Bean.
G- Beryl-Red.
S- Sadr.

Fever

F- Clematis, Holly.
G- Chalcedony, Copper, Coral, Gold, Jasper-Red, Silver.

Fish

F- Bamboo, Bottlebrush, Carob, Coffee, Cosmos, Grapefruit, Motherwort, Sea Lettuce.
G- Aquamarine, Cobaltite, Corals-All, Larimar.
S- M52.

Fleas

F- Aloe Vera, Garlic, Pennyroyal.
G- Diamond-White.

Focus

F- Candy Barrel Cactus, Cholla Cactus, Ephedra, Jumping Cholla Cactus, Madia, Mullein, Staghorn.
G- Clinoptilolite, Cordierite.
E- Neon.

Fur

F- Calliandra, Crab Apple.

Grief/Loss/Despair

F- Amaranthus, Artichoke, Bittersweet, Bleeding Heart, Borage, Cape Honeysuckle, Cucumber, Feverfew, Foxglove, Honeysuckle, Milkmaids, Milkweed, Mulberry, Mustard, Oak, Pansy, Pleurisy Root, Red Bud, Redwood, Star of Bethlehem, Weeping Willow, Wolfberry, Yucca.
G- Brass, Bronze, Carbon Steel, Chromium, Copper, Datolite, Diamond-Pink, Emerald, Gallium, Gold, Herkimer Diamond, Jet, Libethenite, Magnesium, Manganese, Molybdenum, Palladium, Platinum, Pyrite, Pyroxmangite, Quartz-Rose, Quartz-Rutilated, Quartz-White, Rhodocrocite, Ruby, Sapphire, Sarabauite, Sardonyx, Silver, Star Sapphire, Tin, Zinc.
S- Aldebaran, M13, M44, Saturn Nebula, Zeta Cygni.
E- Helium, Oxygen, Ozone, Xenon.
SS- Blue Springs Rock Water, Chalice Well, Full Moon Reflection, Liard Hot Springs, Northern Lights, Tidal Forces.

140

Group Harmony

F- Acacia, Basil, Beech, Candlenut Tree, Canyon Grapevine, Cat's Tail, Curry Leaf Tree, Flame of the Forest, Harebell, Hops, Larkspur, Lemmon's Paintbrush, Macadamia, Melaleuca, One-Sided Winter-green, Pear, Plumbago, Quaking Grass, Rosa Buff Beauty, Sweet Pea, Thistle, Wild Sweet Pea.

G- Amethyst, Broshentite, Chrysoprase, Kasolite, Krupkaite, Mesolite, Phenakite, Scholzite, Willemite.

S- Enif, M46.

Healing Crisis

F- Endive, Mariposa Lily.

Heart

Physical

F- Agave, Agave Yaquiana, Aloe Vera, Blackberry, Borage, Foxglove, Candy Barrel Cactus, Desert Barrel Cactus, Flame of the Forest, Green Bog Orchid, Ocotillo, Queen of the Night, Saguaro, Soapberry, Yucca.

G- Callaghanite, Coral-Red, Garnet-Spessartine, Gold, Kunzite-Pink, Magnesium, Mixite, Petrified Wood, Ruby.

S- Arneb, Asellus Borealis.

E- Xenon.

Emotional

F- Alpine Azalea, Black-Eyed Susan, Bleeding Heart, Borage, California Wild Rose, Calla Lily, Calliandra, Cinnamon, Dracaena, Foxglove, Fuschia, Green Bells of Ireland, Harebell, Hawthorne, Holly, Inmortal, Kamani, Mallow, Maple, Mezereum, Mugwort, Noni, Ocotillo, Passion Flower, Peony, Pink Powder Puff, Raspberry, Rosa Gallica Officinalis, Rosa Macrophylla, Shasta Lily, Sunflower, Sweet Briar, Teddy Bear Cholla Cactus, Tundra Twayblade, Zinnia.

G- Callaghanite, Chrysocolla, Chrysoprase, Diamond-Pink, Emerald, Gold, Heulandite, Peridot, Philipsburgite, Platinum, Quartz-Rose, Rhodocrocite, Ruby, Tourmaline-Watermelon.

S- Dubhe, Sargas, Saturn Nebula.

E- Oxygen, Ozone.

SS- Northern Lights.

Chakra

F- Blazing Star, Borage, Green Fairy Orchid, Lobivia Cactus, Lotus, Mallow, Tea Tree.

G- Callaghanite, Garnet-Spessartine, Gold, Pyroxmangite, Ruby, Torber-nite, Tourmaline-Chrome.

141

S- Asellus Borealis, Tarazed.
SS- Northern Lights.

Hip Dysplasia

F- Papaya.
G- Mixite.
E- Xenon.

HIV

F- Apricot, Celery, Centaury, Chaulmoogra Hydnocarpus, Chestnut Bud, Crab Apple, Macartney Rose, Olive, Pansy, Saguaro, Scleranthus, Star of Bethlehem, Tomato, Walnut.
G- Diamond-Pink, Hematite, Jade, Sodalite.
E- Helium, Neon, Xenon.

Horses

F- Balsam Poplar, Banksia Baxtena, Barley, Beech, Bloodroot, Borage, Carob, Cherry Plum, Chestnut Bud, Cosmos, Dandelion, Feverfew, Holly, Loquat, Madia, Mimulus, Mushroom, Ocotillo, Orange Flame Flower Cactus, Pansy, Pleurisy Root, Rattlesnake Plantain Orchid, Round-Leaved Sundew, Saguaro, Snapdragon, Spirea, Star of Bethlehem, Sweet Chestnut, Vine, Walnut.
G- Barite, Diamond-Pink, Ivory, Lazulite, Philipsburgite, Sarandite.
S- Alphard, Asellus Australis, Rasalhague.

Immune System

F- Andalisa, Bamboo, Cedar, Centaury, Kelp, Lotus, Peach, Queen Anne's Lace, Rice, Tomato, Water Violet, Yerba Santa.
G- Agate-Carnelian, Beryl-Red, Brass, Bronze, Chrysolite, Clay, Cuproskowdilite, Diamond-Pink, Diamond-White, Fluorite, Herkimer Diamond, Kutnahorite, Quartz-Brazilian, Quartz-Rose, Quartz-Smoky, Tourmaline-Black, Woodwardite.
S- Pluto.
E- Argon, Helium, Neon, Ozone, Xenon.
SS- Blue Springs Rock Water, Greenland Ice Cap, Liard Hot Springs, Portage Glacier, Solstice Storm, Squaw Spring Rock Water.

Indoor Animals (Light Deprivation)

F- Alpine Azalea, Balsam Poplar, Calendula, California Buckeye, Cassandra, Catnip, Chiming Bells, Commandra, Corn, Delphinium, Devil's

Club, Dogwood, Elephant's Head, Gardenia, Gilia-Scarlet, Green Bells of Ireland, Green Bog Orchid, Hollyhock, Mesquite, Moschatel, Motherwort, Mountain Pride, Rosa Hardii, Shasta Lily, Soapberry, Stephanotis, Sunflower, Wild Oat.
G- Agate-Moss, Alexandrite, Apophyllite, Artinite, Calcite-Orange, Cavanisite, Chrysoprase, Hancockite, Jasper-Green, Larimar, Malachite, Pyromorphite, Quartz-Citrine, Tunnelite, Turquoise, Vauxite.
S- Helios, Procyon.
E- Carbon Dioxide, Krypton, Nitrogen, Oxygen, Ozone, Xenon.
SS- Blue Springs Rock Water, Solstice Sun, Squaw Spring Rock Water.

Inflammation

F- Crab Apple, Holly, Star of Bethlehem.
G- Copper, Hematite, Obsidian, Pearl, Quartz-White, Sapphire, Silver, Tourmaline-White.
S- Mirfak, Pluto, Theta Aurigae, Zeta Cygni.
E- Argon, Helium, Neon, Ozone, Xenon.
SS- Greenland Ice Cap, Portage Glacier, Squaw Spring Rock Water.

Insomnia

F- Chamomile-German, Chaparral, Morning Glory, Mugwort.
G- Lodestone, Malachite.
E- Carbon Dioxide, Oxygen, Ozone.

Kidneys

F- Bog Blueberry, Bamboo, Blackberry, Irish Moss, Kelp, Rice, Sea Lettuce, Spider Lily, Swamp Onion.
G- Nephrite, Zincite.

Lethargy/Apathy

F- Bignonia, Bog Blueberry, Dog Rose, Gentian, Gorse, Horseradish, Khat, Morning Glory, Olive, Plumbago, Poha, Prickly Wild Rose, Robinia, Sugar Cane, Sycamore, Tea Plant, Wallflower, Wild Ginger, Wild Rose, Zucchini.
G- Agate-Botswana, Alexandrite, Bloodstone, Calcite-Orange, Fluorite, Herkimer Diamond, Opal, Platinum, Sapphire, Spectrolite, Szeniscite.
S- Alludra, Epsilon Persei, Izar, Sargas, Vega.
E- Carbon Dioxide, Krypton, Neon, Oxygen, Ozone, Xenon.
SS- Blue Springs Rock Water, Greenland Ice Cap, Liard Hot Springs, Portage Glacier, Squaw Spring Rock Water.

Leukemia

F- Apricot, Chaulmoogra Hydnocarpus, Lotus, Pansy.
G- Bronze, Chalcedony, Hematite, Ivory, Opal-Light, Sodalite.
S- Alpheratz.
E- Argon, Carbon Dioxide, Krypton, Neon, Oxygen, Ozone, Xenon.
SS- Blue Springs Rock Water, Greenland Ice Cap, Liard Hot Springs, Portage Glacier, Solstice Storm, Solstice Sun, Squaw Spring Rock Water.

Lick Granuloma

F- California Wild Rose, Snapdragon, Yerba Santa.
G- Turquoise.

Light & Color Healing

F- Calendula, Green Bells of Ireland.
G- Agate-Fire, Alexandrite, Artinite, Vauxite.
E- Krypton, Nitrogen, Xenon.
SS- Solstice Storm.

Light Sensitivity

F- Mimulus, Peach.

Liver

F- Almond, Apple, Apricot, Aspen, Avocado, Beech, Blackberry, Cedar, Cherry, Chestnut Bud, Date Palm, Kamani, Locust, Macadamia, Mango, Maple, Nectarine, Oak, Olive, Orange, Redwood.
G- Aquamarine, Creedite, Star Sapphire.
E- Oxygen, Ozone, Xenon.

Lungs

F- Blackberry, Eucalyptus, Yarrow.
G- Brass, Bronze, Carbon Steel, Chromium, Copper, Gallium, Gold, Magnesium, Manganese, Molybdenum, Palladium, Platinum, Sardonyx, Serpentine, Silver, Tin, Zinc.
E- Carbon Dioxide, Oxygen, Ozone, Xenon.
SS- Blue Springs Rock Water, Greenland Ice Cap, Portage Glacier, Solstice Sun, Squaw Spring Rock Water, Tidal Forces.

Mouth, Jaw, Gums, Teeth

F- Banana, Gentian, Grapefruit, Snapdragon.
G- Beryl, Lapis Lazuli, Sarandite, Turquoise.

Music & Sound Therapy (enhancement)

F- Bleeding Heart, Jimson Weed, Pear, Red Mountain Heather.
G- Carletonite, Chabazite, Hemimorphite, Jade, Kinoite, Purpurite, Pyro-morphite, Vauxite.
S- Cheleb, Mirach.
E- Xenon.

Nerve Damage

F- Comfrey.
S- Alpheratz.
E- Ozone, Xenon.
SS- Greenland Ice Cap, Portage Glacier, Solstice Storm.

Nervous System

F- Buffalo Gourd, California Bay Laurel, Coconut, Comfrey, Cotton, Fairy Duster, Ginger, Goldenseal, Heliconia, Hibiscus, Morning Glory, Purple Nightshade.
G- Gold, Silver.
S- Alpheratz.
E- Ozone, Xenon.
SS- Greenland Ice Cap, Portage Glacier, Solstice Storm.

Newborns

F- Almond, Balm of Gilead, Coconut, Crocus, Grove Sandwort, Noni, Northern Ladies Slipper, Onion, Shasta Daisy, Shasta Lily, Spirea.
G- Moonstone, Peridot.
S- Alludra, Asellus Borealis, Epsilon Persei, Schedar, Vega.
E- Neon, Nitrogen, Oxygen, Ozone, Xenon.
SS- Chalice Well, Rainbow Glacier.

Outdoor Animals

F- Bells of Ireland, Pukiawe.

Oversensitivity

F- Asparagus, Beech, Crab Apple, Dutchman's Breeches, Live Forever, One-Sided Wintergreen, Pennyroyal, Sensitive Plant, White Violet, Willow, Yarrow.
G- Clinoclase, Covellite, Crocoite, Moonstone.

Over-Dependency/Attachment

F- Chicory, Milky Nipple Cactus, Oregon Grape Root, Sweet Gale, Wolfberry.
G- Quartzite.

Pain

F- Cherry Plum, Holly, Mallow, Pansy, Purple Nightshade.
G- Clay, Jet, Kunzite, Malachite.
E- Xenon.

Pollution

F- Crab Apple, Hops, St. John's Wort.
G- Clay, Turquoise.
S- Cor Caroli.
E- Argon, Helium, Krypton, Neon, Oxygen, Ozone, Xenon.
SS- Blue Springs Rock Water, Greenland Ice Cap, Liard Hot Springs, Portage Glacier, Solstice Storm, Squaw Spring Rock Water.

Post-Op Recovery

F- Agave, Allamanda, Arnica, Chestnut Bud, Comfrey, Cotton, Cotton Grass, Lungwort, Mariposa Lily, Peony, Saguaro, Star of Bethlehem, Star Tulip, Tagua, Wild Sweet Pea.
G- Aquamarine, Cavanisite, Garnet-Tsavorite, Gold, Jasper-Green, Opal, Opal-Dark, Sarabauite.
S- Betelgeuse, Zeta Cygni.
E- Carbon Dioxide, Helium, Neon, Oxygen, Ozone, Xenon.
SS- Blue Springs Rock Water, Chalice Well, Greenland Ice Cap, Liard Hot Springs, Northern Lights, Panther Spring Rock Water, Portage Glacier, Rainbow Glacier, Solstice Storm, Solstice Sun, Squaw Spring Rock Water.

Psychic Protection

F- Aloe Eru, Aloe Vera, Asparagus, Calendula, Calothamnus Validus, Canyon Grapevine, Chaulmoogra Hydnocarpus, Comfrey, Dutch-

man's Breeches, Lotus, Mountain Pennyroyal, Pennyroyal, Tansy, Wormwood, Yarrow.
G- Ferberite, Quartz-White, Turquoise, Vanadanite.
S- Mirfak, Pluto.
E- Argon, Krypton, Neon, Ozone, Xenon.
SS- Greenland Ice Cap, Portage Glacier, Solstice Sun, Squaw Spring Rock Water.

Regeneration

F- Bells of Ireland, Chiming Bells, Fireweed, Rosa Christata, Rosa Horrida, Sweetgrass.
G- Cuproskowdilite, Eilat Stone, Fluorite, Gold, Kutnahorite, Opal, Platinum, Quartz-Rutilated, Silver.
S- Alludra, Alpheratz, Dubhe.
E- Ozone, Xenon.
SS- Blue Springs Rock Water.

Reptiles

F- Goldenseal, Mariposa Lily, Redwood, Yucca.

Respiratory Problems

F- Blackberry, Eucalyptus, Holly, Jasmine, Lobelia.
G- Agate-Carnelian, Jasper-Green.
E- Carbon Dioxide, Oxygen, Ozone, Xenon.
SS- Tidal Forces.

Rodents

F- Black-Eyed Susan, Cedar, Devil's Club.

Service & Therapy Animals

F- Butterfly Lily, Calothamnus Validus, Cedar, Chamomile, Chaparral, Chaulmoogra Hydnocarpus, Clematis, Coconut, Coffee, Cohosh-Black, Cosmos, Cotton, Cow Parsnip, Date Palm, Desert Barrel Cactus, Dutchman's Breeches, Elecampagne, Ephedra, Eucalyptus, Gentian, Ginger, Gingko Biloba, Gotu Kola, Grape, Grapefruit, Grass of Parnassus, Green Fairy Orchid, Gum Plant, Harebell, Hawthorne, Hibiscus, Jade Vine, Jumping Cholla Cactus, Ladies Slipper, Larkspur, Lavender, Lemon Balm, Lemon's Paintbrush, Lettuce, Lime, Lobivia Cactus, Lotus, Macadamia, Mallow, Maple, Marjoram, Melaleuca, Melon Loco, Monkeyflower Bush, Monkey Tail, Morning Glory,

Mountain Pennyroyal, Mullein, Noni, Okra, One-Sided Wintergreen, Orange, Papaya, Parsley, Partridgeberry, Passion Flower, Pear, Pecan, Pennyroyal, Peony, Periwinkle, Pink Tecoma, Poke Weed, Pomegranate, Prickly Pear Cactus, Radish, Raspberry, Roses-All, Sage, Sorrel, Swamp Onion, Thistle, Tomato, Tree Peony, Trumpet Vine, Wallflower, Walnut, Wild Oat, Wisteria, Wormwood, Yarrow, Yerba Santa, Zinnia, Zucchini.

G- Anapoite, Aventurine, Broshentite, Callaghanite, Celestite, Covellite, Diamond-Pink, Dumortierite, Fluorite, Garnet-Spessartine, Gold, Hematite, Heulandite, Jade, Jarosite, Kasolite, Kinoite, Kunzite, Kutnahorite, Lapis Lazuli, Mesolite, Phenakite, Quartz-Brazilian, Quartz-Citrine, Quartz-Rose, Quartz-Smoky, Quartz-White, Rhodocrocite, Ruby, Sarabauite, Silver, Sodalite, Torbernite, Tourmaline-Black, Turquoise.

S- Asellus Borealis, Dubhe, Enif, Epsilon Persei, Izar, M13, Mintaka, Rasalhague, Scheat, Schedar, Tarazed, Vega.

E- Argon, Carbon Dioxide, Helium, Hydrogen, Krypton, Neon, Nitrogen, Oxygen, Ozone, Xenon.

SS- Blue Springs Rock Water, Greenland Ice Cap, Liard Hot Springs, Northern Lights, Panther Spring Rock Water, Portage Glacier, Rainbow Glacier, Squaw Spring Rock Water.

Skin

F- Beech, Cedar, Luffa, Rice, Spider Lily.
G- Garnet-Rhodolite, Kutnahorite, Onyx, Pyrite.
S- Mirfak.
E- Helium, Ozone, Xenon.
SS- Blue Springs Rock Water, Greenland Ice Cap, Liard Hot Springs, Portage Glacier.

Snakes

F- Rattlesnake Plantain Orchid.
G- Amethyst.

Spay & Neuter Recovery

F- Comfrey, Easter Lily, Evening Primrose, Forget Me Not, Lotus, Mariposa Lily, Orchid, Pansy, Peony, Rose, Squash, Star of Bethlehem, Star Tulip, Sunflower, Tiger Lily, Wood Betony.
G- Jasper-Green, Opal-Dark.
S- Alpheratz, Betelgeuse, Epsilon Persei, Helios, Mirfak, Zeta Cygni.
E- Neon, Oxygen, Ozone, Xenon.

SS- Blue Springs Rock Water, Chalice Well, Greenland Ice Cap, Liard Hot Springs, Northern Lights, Panther Spring Rock Water, Portage Glacier, Rainbow Glacier, Squaw Spring Rock Water, Tidal Forces.

Spine/Back

F- Banana, Coconut, Heliconia, Indian Pipe, Lilac.
G- Coral-Black, Coral-Red.
E- Neon.

Spraying (Cats)

F- Black Spruce.

Stomach

F- Aloe Vera, Cotton, Loquat, Papaya, Potato, Red Mountain Heather.

Stress

F- Bamboo, Black-Eyed Susan, Bottlebrush, Butterfly Lily, Cacao, Catnip, Chamomile, Cherry Plum, Clove Tree, Cotton, Dahlia, Dandelion, Dill, Elecampagne, Elm, Fennel, Figwort, Freesia, Ginseng, Grapefruit, Grape Hyacinth, Henna, Hibiscus, Holly, Hyssop, Indian Pipe, Kiwi, Licorice, Lobelia, Loquat, Maltese Cross, Milkweed, Noni, Oak, Okra, Orchid, Pleurisy Root, Red Rugosa Rose, Rice, Rosa Corymbifera, Rosa Gallica Officinalis, Self-Heal, Sensitive Plat, Sorrel, Stinging Nettle, Sycamore, Valerian, Yarrow, Yerba Santa, Ylang Ylang, Zinnia.
G- Agate-Carnelian, Atacamite, Aventurine, Chrysocolla, Cuproskowdilite, Dioptase, Durangite, Herkimer Diamond, Jet, Moonstone, Pearl, Pyrite, Silver, Tourmaline-Black.
S- Alpheratz.
E- Helium.
SS- Squaw Spring Rock Water.

Studs

F- Balsam Poplar, Banksia Baxtena, Bottlebrush, Squash.
G- Beryl-Red.

Tissue Regeneration

F- Bells of Ireland, Rosa Christata, Rosa Horrida.
G- Aegerine, Copper, Cuproskowdilite, Gold, Rhodocrocite, Silver.

S- Alpheratz.
E- Xenon.

Toxicity

F- Canyon Grapevine, Crab Apple, Hop Tree, Mountain Pennyroyal, Noni, St. John's Wort.
G- Chrysolite, Clay, Diamond, Nephrite, Quartz-Smoky, Tourmaline-Black, Turquoise, Woodwardite.
S- Cor Caroli, Helios, Izar, Mirfak, Pluto, Zeta Cygni.
E- Argon, Carbon Dioxide, Helium, Krypton, Neon, Ozone, Xenon.
SS- Blue Springs Rock Water, Greenland Ice Cap, Portage Glacier, Solstice Storm, Solstice Sun, Squaw Spring Rock Water.

Training

F- Avocado, Bear Grass, Black Spruce, Butterfly Lily, Cayenne, Chestnut Bud, Coffee, Cosmos, Crab Apple, Forget Me Not, Gladiola, Grapefruit, Hairy Butterwort, Lemon, Madia, Marigold-French, Mullein, Mushroom, Poha, Saguaro, Shasta Daisy, Sitka Burnett, Whitethorn, White Chestnut, Yerba Mate.
G- Gordonite, Ivory, Lodestone, Platinum, Tremolite.
E- Hydrogen.
SS- Glacier River, Greenland Ice Cap, Squaw Spring Rock Water.

Transition

F- Allamanda, Aspen, California Pitcher Plant, Carob, Cat's Tail, Chestnut Bud, Cow Parsnip, Crocus, Dill, Echinacea, Evening Primrose, Forget Me Not, Grove Sandwort, Helleborus-Black, Henbane, Henna, Klein's Pencil Cholla Cactus, Magnolia, Mariposa Lily, Mugwort, Prickly Pear, Red Rugosa Rose, Redwood, Round Leaved Sundew, Saguaro, Shasta Lily, Single Delight, Snowplant, Spirea, Staghorn Cholla Cactus, Summer Snowflake, Sweet Flag, Thurber's Gilia, Tree Opuntia, Walnut, Wolfberry.
G- Aventurine, Clinoptilolite, Okenite, Peridot, Quartz-Brazilian, Scholzite.
SS- Glacier River, Greenland Ice Cap, Polar Ice, Rainbow Glacier, Squaw Spring Rock Water, Tidal Forces.

Travel

F- Corn-Sweet, Dandelion, Dill, Foxglove, Labrador Tea, Licorice, Loquat, Rhododendron, Sea Lettuce, Summer Snowflake, Yerba Santa, Ylang Ylang.
G- Chrysocolla, Dumortierite, Quartz-Smoky, Tourmaline-Black.

E- Neon, Xenon.
SS- Liard Hot Springs, Polar Ice Cap, Portage Glacier, Rainbow Glacier, Squaw Spring Rock Water.

Trust Issues

F- Agave, Aspen, Avocado, Bamboo Orchid, Birch, Bleeding Heart, Bog Rosemary, California Wild Rose, Compass Barrel Cactus, Ephedra, Evening Primrose, French Marigold, Klein's Pencil Cholla Cactus, Mariposa Lily, Morning Glory, Oregon Grape Root, Pansy, Prickly Wild Rose, Queen Anne's Lace, Saguaro, St. John's Wort, Sweet Pea, Tiger Lily, White Violet.
G- Broshentite, Diamond-Pink, Star Sapphire.
S- M44.
E- Oxygen, Ozone.
SS- Tidal Forces.

Tumors

F- Eggplant, Holly.
G- Agate-Botswana, Gallium, Herkimer Diamond, Jet.
E- Argon.
SS- Full Moon Reflection, Greenland Ice Cap, Portage Glacier.

Vaccine Induced Illness/Reaction

F- Apple, Birch, Blackberry, Bleeding Heart, Bottlebrush, Cedar, Centaury, Coconut, Comfrey, Coralroot-Spotted, Cow Parsnip, Crab Apple, Garlic, Lilac, Noni, Passion Flower, Pine Drops, Rose, Sage, Whitethorn, Zinnia, Zucchini.
G- Agate-Moss, Berthierite, Bloodstone, Gold, Kutnahorite, Moldavite, Moonstone, Nephrite, Opal-Dark, Silver, Turquoise, Woodwardite, Zincite.
S- Alpheratz, Izar, Mirfak, Pluto, Zeta Cygni.
E- Neon, Oxygen, Ozone, Xenon.
SS- Greenland Ice Cap, Liard Hot Springs, Portage Glacier, Solstice Storm.

Vomiting

F- Chamomile, Rock Rose.
G- Kunzite, Talc.

Wandering

F- Sweet Pea.

Weight Loss

F- Impatiens.
G- Coral-Red.
E- Ozone, Xenon.

Wild Animals

F- Aspen, Banksia Baxtena, Blackberry, Bo Tree, Cerato, Chamomile, Edelweiss, Foxglove, Manzanita, Mesquite, Shasta Daisy, Shasta Lily, Sweet Briar.
G- Tiger's Eye.
S- Sargas.
E- Nitrogen, Oxygen, Ozone, Xenon.
SS- Blue Springs Rock Water, Liard Hot Springs, Northern Lights, Squaw Spring Rock Water, Tidal Forces.

Wounds

F- Angelica, Comfrey, Evening Primrose, Mariposa Lily.
G- Chabazite, Hematite, Jade, Jasper-Green.
S- Zeta Cygni.
E- Xenon.
SS- Blue Springs Rock Water, Chalice Well, Liard Hot Springs, Northern Lights, Portage Glacier, Rainbow Glacier.

Part Three

Energy Healing Modalities and Technology

Energetic Aromatherapy

Aromatherapy is quickly becoming one of the most popular healing modalities of our day. Though it may seem new, the power and affect that fragrance has had on all living creatures has been well known for centuries. Today we can go into most supermarkets and find "aromatherapy" candles and incense. Most of these products contain synthetic chemicals and substances, with little natural ingredients or benefit. Aromatic essential oils that are pure come from plants and flowers without any adulteration (additives) or chemical processing. Pure aromatic oils are more expensive than synthetics or synthetic blends, as it can take hundreds of pounds of some flowers to produce an ounce of oil. However, there is no comparison in quality.

Aromatherapy affects all beings in various ways. When applied topically, taken orally (under supervision of a qualified practitioner), or micro-diffused, they are absorbed through the tissues into the bloodstream. The oils benefit the physical body, providing anti-fungal, antibiotic, and analgesic benefits, to name a few. When essential oils are experienced through the sense of smell (olfactory system), the benefits are primarily mental and emotional. The olfactory nerve is stimulated, which has a direct relationship to the limbic system of the brain. Odor stimuli in the limbic system release neurotransmitters, which reduce pain, promote euphoria and bring peace of mind. They can calm, stimulate and balance, as well as awaken sexuality. The spiritual and emotional aspects of essential oils, the synthesis of sun and plant, are the vibrational qualities, which I term *energetic aromatherapy*. This aspect of aromatherapy primarily affects the chakras and the energy systems.

The quality of vibration carried through pure aromatic oils resonates on the etheric level. This vibrational aspect is borne of the highest life energy and consciousness of the plant, particularly when the oils are made from flowers. Just as the physical herb, when taken internally mainly affects the physical body, and vibrational remedies resonate with the etheric bodies, the vibrational qualities of infused aromatherapy oils affect the vibrational bodies. The doctrine of signatures that is applicable to flowers and gemstones, for instance, is also a valuable tool in understanding the correlation of essential oils to specific chakras, the five elements and the energy systems of all creatures. Often the qualities of the essences derived from plants, trees and flowers are very similar to those of the aromatic oils.

When utilizing aromatherapy for animals, it is important to remember that they have a sense of smell that is often several hundred times stronger than humans. Essential oils are potently concentrated and should be used sparingly. Often, just one or two drops will do. Keep the aroma source away from where the animal eats. Be sure to keep the home well ventilated. Also, aromatherapy oils are powerful. They are often toxic in their concentrated form. Always keep them out of the reach of children and animals.

Methods of Application

The very best way for animals to experience the healing aromas of nature is to plant fresh flowers and grasses just for them in a special part of the yard, field or garden. If this is not possible, or during the winter months, the best method for application of essential oils is through a heatless micro-diffuser. The oils are finely misted into the air. This method of delivery is more expensive, but the most effective, as the oils are not heated and the beneficial aromatic properties are not altered in any way.

Less expensive and still very effective are heat diffusers and heat lamps, some of which use open flame. Use the same precaution here that you would with candles, and keep out of the reach of children and inquisitive animals. Also, never leave them unattended while burning.

If open flame is a problem or inconvenience in your household, or for aromatherapy while you sleep, there are several electrical devices available. These are small, effective and mostly inexpensive.

Some plug into electrical outlets or car cigarette lighters, which can greatly aid animal transport.

Also, freshly harvested or purchased organic fragrant herbs, such as lavender, lemon or mint, can be made into sachets or stuffed animal toys for their bedding. A pouch sewn into the collar can work well as a flea repellant. Or just a drop or two on a cotton ball in the bed, cat carrier or on the bedding can aid in sleep, stress or illness.

For flea infestation, an essential oil flea dip can be used, with 10 drops of oil (depending upon size of the animal) in the water. As a flea and pest spray, ten drops of cedar, tea tree, lavender, eucalyptus or citronella in 1 tablespoon oil (almond or olive) and a cup of warm water work well in a spray bottle. Shake well.

For livestock, farm and outdoor animals, an excellent way to offer aroma is with a spray bottle, filled with the essential oil and pure water. Seven to ten drops in the bottle is sufficient. A few mists even several feet away can help animals to relax and calm, give them stamina through any kind of labor, and clear the air of stress and trauma.

In ancient times, huge cauldrons of boiling herbs were placed near horses and livestock to treat colic and pneumonia. Though not exactly convenient today, with electrical access, humidifiers can be used for the same purpose. Because it is an electrical appliance that is used outdoors, it must be sheltered safely. Cold or hot air humidifiers can be used with pungent oils, such as camphor or eucalyptus, to promote respiratory health.

When to Use Aromatherapy

Any time an animal is stressed in any way, all parts of him will suffer. The mental, emotional and physical aspects of an animal's being are much more closely interfaced than humans. Therefore, when addressing your cat's sneezes and runny nose, for instance, it is important to address the emotional discomfort that goes along with it.

Whenever an animal is exposed to any tension, change or upset in his life, he will benefit from aromatherapy. Even if he seems just a little out of sorts, aromatic oils can work wonders.

Essential oils can cleanse, purify, uplift, relax, and support animals at all levels, sometimes all at once! And everyone in the home receives their healing benefits.

Aromatherapy isn't just for upset and stress. It can enhance an already balanced and happy home, by providing a gentle lift or boost of energy. Just as a springtime bouquet of flowers can be the perfect addition to a beautiful home, the lovely blend of aromas gathered from nature can take one's attitude (animal or human) to new heights.

The Magic of Lavender

For centuries throughout the world, lavender has been revered and adored for its soothing and healing properties. Few creations of nature carry such powerful healing qualities in such graceful, beautiful form. The oil of lavender has antibiotic, anti-viral and anti-fungal properties. It is used widely throughout Europe and England by doctors and practitioners for treating external and internal infection. Lavender oil repairs damaged skin and accelerates growth and healing of new skin. It is an anti-spasmodic and analgesic, a sedative as well as stimulant, and anti-depressant. Lavender kills germs, and can be used as an antiseptic and diuretic. It treats headaches, lethargy, depression and fatigue. For animals that are feeling out of sorts, or recovering from surgery or a kennel stay, it can help to welcome them home and back into their body. It eases hypertension, insomnia, muscle aches and pains, and is good to use with massage. Well-diluted high-quality oil of lavender in pure water can be used with eye discharge and infection, as well as bites, bruises and burns. Lavender is an excellent flea repellant, and can be put into the rinse water of a bath, or diluted and sprayed on animals directly. When puppies have found an inappropriate area to chew, claw or scratch-be it furniture, carpet, or whatever-a few drops of lavender rubbed into the spot will deter them safely and successfully. Also, once a cat or dog has urinated in the house, straight lavender oil or a strong lavender/water solution applied directly on the cleaned area, can absorb all smell and keep them from returning to the same spot.

For female dogs and cats in heat, the pervasive aroma of lavender has the ability to mask the scent and keep the males off-track. For animals often left alone in the home, the aroma of lavender can be very supportive. Place a few drops in the dishwasher and turn on the drying cycle just before you leave, to let the aroma safely steam throughout the house. Also, lavender seed in the bedding itself is an excellent flea deterrent.

Above all, plant lavender in your yard, garden or pots for the windowsill. Animals love to smell it, walk through it, and sleep in it. The smell of fresh lavender will provide spiritual nourishment and upliftment for everyone in the home.

Aromatherapy
Oil Qualities

Angelica- For abuse, trauma, post-op recovery and anxiety. Balancing and grounding.

Balm- Soothing for allergies, insomnia, depression, nervous tension and stress. Good for anger and hostility. Balances, protects and energizes.

Bergamot- Calms anxiety, stress, and nervousness. Lifts depression. Excellent balancer.

Black Pepper- Excellent for restoring boundaries. Provides protection. Excellent in many combinations. Not to be used near pregnant or nursing animals.

Camphor- Excellent oil in treatment of bronchitis, pneumonia and colic. Not good to blend with vibrational remedies.

Cedar- Allays fear, anger, nervous anxiety and disassociation. Protects and cleanses the aura and the environment. Excellent for sickness and trauma, during and after. Comforting, calming and uplifting. Insect repellant. Good flea spray and dip.

Cedarwood- Balancing and strengthening to lower chakras and the energy field. Not to be used near pregnant or nursing animals.

Chamomile- Allays anger, over-sensitivity, and depression. Calming during pregnancy and birth. Balancing and nourishing.

Cinnamon- For depression, lethargy and apathy. Warming, comforting and uplifting. Not to be used near pregnant or nursing animals.

Citronella- Insect repellant. Excellent flea spray or dip.

Clary Sage-Cleansing, balancing and inspiring. Calming for animals in heat. Good for spay and neuter recovery. Not to be used near pregnant or nursing animals.

Cypress- A cleansing and protective oil. Supports the energy field.

Dill- Excellent nervous system tonic. Restorative, uplifting and balancing.

Eucalyptus- Excellent for stress and trauma, assisting in the release of grief and the restoration of full, normal breathing and oxygenation of the body. Indicated for respiratory distress, pneumonia, kennel cough, and colic. Calming and restorative. Enables the body to receive more life-energy. Good flea spray and dip. Not good to blend with vibrational remedies.

Fennel- Nerve tonic. Reduces stress and nervousness. Excellent for animals who are subjected to cigarette smoke. Neutralizes toxicity in body. Not to be used near pregnant or nursing animals.

Frankincense- Balancing and energizing to chakras and energy field.

Geranium- Anti-depressant. Uplifting.

Grapefruit- Good for depression, lethargy and sadness. Lightens spirit and promotes well-being.

Hyssop- For toxicity or stress of any kind. A good overall cleanser. Balances emotions. Not to be used near pregnant or nursing animals.

Jasmine- Excellent oil for abuse and trauma recovery. For depression, fear, lack of self-esteem. Lifts spirit and lightens the heart. Balances and activates chakras and energy field. Just a little bit will do!

Juniper- Indicated for weakness and anxiety. Excellent for recovery. Detoxifies and uplifts, purifies on all levels. Cleanses the environment. Not to be used near pregnant or nursing animals.

Lavender- Excellent for depression, stress, anger and imbalance. Stimulates healing, provides nurturance and balance, calming to nervous system. Energetic cleanser to all systems as well as the environment. Refreshing. Brings nature indoors. Anti-inflammatory. Excellent flea spray and dip.

Lemon Grass- Remedy for malaise, lethargy and crankiness. Refreshing and uplifting.

Lemon Verbena- Uplifting and stabilizing during labor and birth. Provides light-heartedness. Encourages stamina and inner strength. Carries very high frequency of light and joy.

Lily of the Valley- Heart strengthener on all levels.

Marjoram- For anxiety, hostility, stress, agitation. Acts as a sedative. Relaxing. Not to be used near pregnant or nursing animals.

Mint- Excellent for fatigue and lethargy. Refreshing and gently stimulating.

Myrrh- Energizing and balancing to the chakras and energy field. Not to be used near pregnant or nursing animals.

Neroli- Excellent first-aid remedy. For shock, trauma, and abuse recovery. Eases fear and depression. Excellent chakra and energy field balancer.

Orange- For sadness, and animals who are overly seeking affection and attention. For anxiousness and nervousness. Uplifts, relieves stress, relaxes and nurtures.

Peppermint- For gastric upset and respiratory problems, such as kennel cough. Allays itching. Not to be used near pregnant or nursing animals.

Rockrose- For withdrawal and aloofness, especially in cats. Nurturing and balancing.

Rose- Excellent for deep sorrow, grief, emotional pain and separation. Uplifts and strengthens heart chakra, opens the entire being to the love of God and nature. The supreme balancer, bringing patience and warming calm. Balances and energizes chakras, especially heart, and the energy fields.

Rosemary- For poor boundaries, low self-confidence from trauma, abuse or aggressive animals or children. Indicated for heart problems, liver disease and stomach upset. Good for post-op recovery. Strengthening, uplifting and stimulating to brain and nervous system. Good for training, stimulates mental body. Not to be used near pregnant or nursing animals.

Rosewood- Balancing and strengthening to blood and lower chakras, as well as the energy field. Excellent in jojoba dilution for the skin.

Sage- **Not recommended for animals. The oil can trigger epileptic seizures. Unsafe for pregnant and nursing animals.**

Sandalwood- Excellent for anxiety, stress, isolation, aggression and withdrawal. Primary oil for psychic protection and grounding. Wonderful in almost all combinations. Indicated for group harmony and family situations. Emotionally calming. Soothing and balancing after spay and neuter surgery, or trauma recovery.

Sea Pine- Heals residual trauma, especially from sickness and surgery recovery. Cleansing and detoxifying.

Tea Tree- Disinfectant, anti-fungal and anti-bacterial. Good flea spray or dip.

Thyme- Excellent respiratory oil, especially indicated for pneumonia. Not to be used near pregnant or nursing animals.

Vetiver- For nervousness, stress, disinterest in food, disconnectedness. Grounding, strengthening and regenerating.

Yarrow- Excellent oil for animals who are in a toxic or stressful environment. Helps to alleviate stress from feuding people and negative energy by balancing and supporting psychic energies of all concerned.

Ylang Ylang- Excellent for abuse, trauma and injury. Also indicated for fear, anger, self-esteem issues, nervousness, depression and aggressive outbursts. Relieves inner tension. Balancing and uplifting, provides core support.

Light, Color
and Nature Healing

The importance of light in the health and well being of all living creatures is essential. Natural sunlight is the key factor in pineal health, and the pineal regulates all other glands and energy systems. Correct pineal function is essential for mental, physical and emotional balance, which keeps animals happy, at peace, and free from gloom, depression and lethargy. The pineal gland also regulates sleep, appetite and hormone function. Animals who are indoors the vast majority of the time do not receive sunlight or full spectral light and therefore have compromised pineal function. It is important to provide a lifestyle for *all* of our animals that includes some daylight each and every day. The importance of moonlight in proper pineal and energetic health has not been researched anywhere, to my knowledge, particularly in regard to animals. Yet the lunar influence has a key part to play for every living being. Wolves love to howl at the moon, and share a special attunement to it. Animals may want to get out of the house at night solely for this purpose: to howl at, gaze upon or simply bathe in the light of the moon.

Color is simply the differentiation of light. Each color carries a specific frequency to energize, vibrate with and balance all aspects of an animal's being. The individual chakras, energy systems and corresponding organs, areas of body, cellular structure and areas of the brain are affected and stimulated by color. Color being energy, its influence on the energetic bodies can be immediate and profound.

Color therapy as a tool for balance and healing is relatively simple for animals to assimilate. Even highly domesticated indoor animals have a deep attunement to nature, her rhythms and colors.

It is a key part of their make-up. Sunlight, if blocked through glass, will not have full spectral effect. Direct exposure to sunlight, either outside or through an open window or door, is the best medicine for all animals that are out of balance, physically or emotionally. Light devices can also be effective for the seriously ill, traumatized or post-op animal. On the contrary, lights in the home that are not full-spectrum can actually have negative impact on the energetic field of animals, eventually compromising the immune system.

For animals, perhaps even more so than humans, the light of the sun contains every color and frequency necessary for healing. There are times when specific colors can be advantageous, particularly when animals are not able to be outside due to surgery recovery or sickness. A color chart on the following page gives specific healing qualities for each color. Color healing is simple, easy and immediately effective. It also can be done long distance, while the animal is in the vet hospital or kenneled, for instance. With the animal in front of you, (or visualize her there) surround her with white light. Intuit or dowse a color that feels appropriate for the animals needs, or pick one from the chart below. Feel the color through your own body, breathing it in on the inhale, out on the exhale. Then let the intense *feeling* of the color radiate from your heart to your animals, in through their breath, out through their breath. Feel the healing color flow from your hands to her body. Let the color wash through the animal, bringing in specific life force on the inhale, cleansing out pain and blockages on the exhale. After just a few minutes, you will feel or even see a difference in the way she looks. Only 2-5 minutes are necessary for this color balancing to work. It may be necessary to repeat a few times daily.

Another way that the color chart can be used is for burning candles with the specific intent of healing. Burning a candle with the specific color needed, for a few hours or even minutes, can assist our animal friends greatly. Be sure to never leave the candle alone, and always trim the wick to ¼ inch before burning.

COLOR CHART

COLOR	BODY ASSOCIATIONS	QUALITIES	ANTIDOTE
White	All of body	Cleansing, energizing	None needed
Gold	All of body	Purifying, energizing	None needed
Violet	Skeleton, pineal, nerves, brain	Purifying, strengthening	Yellow
Indigo	Lymph system, pituitary, eyes, pain	Relaxing, detoxifying	Orange
Blue	Inflammation, ears, throat, mouth	Cooling, relaxing, balancing	Red
Green	Heart, tissue, thymus	Balancing, soothing, regenerating	None needed
Yellow	Digestion, liver, stomach, ulcers	Uplifting, energizing	Violet
Orange	Spleen, bladder, pancreas, kidneys	Detoxifying, activating	Indigo/Blue
Red	Blood, spine, sex organs	Stimulating, energizing	Blue
Pink	Heart, emotional upset, anxiety	Soothing, calming	Turquoise
Turquoise	Wounds, headache, fever	Cooling, soothing	Pink

The healing qualities of nature and her elements are a great gift to our animal creatures. We humans can only guess at the intimate relationship that they share. The hidden smells and sounds that animals can catch in the wind invigorate and renew their spirit. This natural instinctive affinity with the outdoors can be driven out to a great degree, and the more it is, the more neurotic the animal. On the physical level alone, the earth, rain, sun, wind and even snow can keep them healthy. A run along the beach or lakeshore can keep them happy. When the entire realm of angelic and devic nature spirits is considered, it becomes clear that their entire being *must* be exposed to nature for their complete health and invisible guidance. The essences of flowers, gems, starlights and the elements can activate this connection and enhance it. But there is equal need for our animal friends to experience it through all of their senses. Walking a dog on a leash on a busy street is not allowing them an intimate relationship with nature. Provide a lifestyle for your animals that encourages the whole family to be outdoors and in the wild whenever possible. Even small city parks can be a refuge for all who live hectic lives on the highways and indoors much of the time. Dialoging with the sweet spirits of nature beats the drone of the television any day of the week. It's important for all of us to make time to experience the balance and healing of Mother nature.

Sound Healing

"All that takes place in nature is permeated with a mysterious music
which is the earthly projection of the music of the spheres.
In every plant and in every animal there is really incorporated
a tone of the music of the spheres."
—Rudolph Steiner

Animals attune to frequency naturally. Most animal species can hear pitches that are entirely out of the range of human hearing, and are sensitive to energies that are carried on these super-frequencies. As limited as we humans are by our own narrow bands of perception, when we begin to open the door of verbal communication with our animal friends, the entire sound spectrum becomes available to us in many ways, even though we may not "hear" the specific notes.

Many large mammals, such as the rhinoceros, elephant and whale, vocalize sound at much lower pitch than humans can generate, or even hear. Sometimes, we humans can *feel* the vibration of these low, infrasound frequencies. High notes in the sound spectrum, while out of range of human hearing, can be heard by many kinds of animals.

One of the most simple and profound ways to vocally communicate with animals is to sing. Our spoken voice can be very soothing and reassuring to our companions, but soft singing can be profoundly comforting. Our animals don't care how well we sing or even if we're in tune. They are nourished from the love that we are offering from our heart to theirs, through the beautiful medium of the human voice. When a loving, trusting relationship has been established between a person and animal, a deeper attunement is possible by holding them close and singing soft words of comfort and upliftment. Just singing their names to them, with love and caring intent, can be deeply healing.

Over the years, I have developed close relationships with dogs that carry pain and psychic overload in their bodies. Through our bond of trust, I have been able to sing penetrating tones into their heart, with my mouth right up against their chest, to assist them in releasing emotional and physical stress and heartache. Often, I ease into it, starting with soft low tones, and then gradually get louder, using higher pitched pulsating tones. If the dog is vocal by nature, he will often join in with me, howling to match my pitch, actively participating in the release. Afterwards, he is often thankful and visibly lightened. It creates an even more intimate bond, when it becomes clear that we can speak their language.

All creatures love beautiful and soothing music, especially acoustic harp, violin, flute and piano. This is extremely beneficial during times of recovery or stress, in a new home or surrounding, or to create a harmonious and tranquil atmosphere for new family members. Drumming music that is rhythmic (but not overly percussive) can be very effective, as this helps to restore body and breathing rhythms. Animals attune easily to soft vocal music with light lyrical voices and pastoral orchestration. In particular, for animals who are recovering from any kind of trauma, music that has close to the same tempo as the animal's normal heart rate (see chart next page), can have a very grounding and balancing affect. For musical selections that ease stress and provide calm, please see Appendix B.

For those who are musically inclined, musical instruments can be a powerful and wonderful way to broadcast the energy of vibrational remedies. A few drops of rose quartz elixir, for instance, placed inside a piano, or in the sound box of a guitar or violin, will bring the energy of unconditional love into the room *through* the instrument. This is true for most instruments, to allow the music to take the vibrational remedy's qualities and broadcast them inside the note frequency. It can be felt through the body and is an excellent way to experience these essences more deeply.

Each chakra, or energy center in an animal's body has a corresponding soul note. (See Chakra Chart in The Energetic Systems of Animals chapter.) Sounding the note vocally or with a musical instrument, chime or tuning fork can be beneficial for the animal's energy system. When a chakra is out of balance due to depletion or overload, the frequency, or corresponding note value, becomes stressed. The sounding of the specific note of that chakra resonates with the natural frequency, and harmonizes the energy within that center. This has a pervasive balancing affect through the organs and areas of the body that are related to that chakra, as well as to the animal's whole being. When approaching the animal in a gentle and comforting way, the appropriate note can be sounded close to the body, with immediate effect.

The following chart gives the normal resting heart range rate of each animal species in beats per minute. Music tempo that is matched to the target average of the animal can have calming and balancing effect. This chart serves as a guide only, as breeds within each species can vary tremendously by size and weight. You can find your animals normal rate by checking it when she is at rest a few times and taking the average.

Also, smaller domestic birds, reptiles and rodents have heart rates which range from a several beats per minute to several hundred per minute. It would probably be safe to say that any music with a soothing rhythm and melody to humans would have positive effect on all creatures in the home.

HEART RATE CHART

ANIMAL	HEART RATE RANGE
Horses	23-70
Dolphins	60-70
Dogs	40-140
Cats	110-140
Birds of Prey	310-410

Electromagnetic Pollution & Healing with Crystal Grids

We all live amidst energy: above us, all around us, in the ground beneath our feet and even through our very bodies. And not all of it is beneficial. Electrical and overhead wiring, power and telephone lines, transformer power stations and towers, radar and microwave towers, computers, televisions, motors and household appliances, cellular phones, electric blankets and fluorescent lights all wreak havoc on the electrical and energy fields of living things. These toxic fields disrupt the natural frequency and charge of the electromagnetic fields in the Planet herself, creating great disruption of harmony and health in all living things. Extensive research has been done on the danger of these fields to humans in the United States, Europe, Canada, Sweden and Russia. *Random electromagnetic field radiation (EMF) is estimated to be about 100 million times stronger today than it was in 1940.* Sweden, perhaps the worlds leading country in EMF research, has conducted extensive tests for decades, and now considers any levels above 3 milligaus as a Class II carcinogen, along with tobacco.

Symptoms of EMF pollution often include disturbed sleep patterns, fatigue, irritability, and compromised immune system. However, it is extremely unusual to find even holistic veterinarians who are aware of this hazard. The best thing for people to do, especially parents and animal caretakers, is learn the dangers and protect your family. (See Bibliography.)

Sources of E.M.F.

The most perilous, toxic locations have proven to be in houses very close to electrical transformers (black or gray cylinders mounted on power poles), and under high-powered electrical wires. Generator plants, power stations and towers should be *miles* from civilization for safety, instead of in our backyards and over our very heads. Inside the home, electrical energy from clock radios, televisions, electronic equipment and computers should be kept at least two feet away for limited exposure, and ten feet away from where you and your animals sleep. Electric blankets are extremely dangerous, and put out deadly levels of magnetic-field toxicity. Animals who sleep on top of beds with electric blankets (human or animal) or waterbed heaters are every bit as vulnerable as the people who do. The same danger is present with electrically heated pads for dog beds. This affects the body by weakening the energy field, compromising the immune system, and often leading to a myriad of immune-system diseases and auto-immune dysfunction. The research indicates high occurrences of leukemia and several cancers from toxic exposure of this kind, especially among children. To my knowledge, **no** research of any kind, in any country, has been done on the impact of electromagnetic fields on animals, but it is safe to assume they are at tremendous risk.

Additionally, there is held in the Earth herself, poison from toxic waste and leakage from industrial and nuclear waste, as well as impure drinking, well and ground water. Deadly energy can be felt in many areas of the planet. Many sites in the West, where Native American and military massacres occurred still hold their deadly charge. The civil war battle sites of Gettysburg and Bull Run are just two examples. Living in or near these potent fields of unresolved poisonous pockets can contribute tremendously to imbalance and ill health.

Effective ways of diffusing E.M.F. are by using magnetic therapy, which is covered in the next chapter, and by placing crystal grids and layouts.

Crystal Layouts and Grids

The energy of stones and crystals has been used throughout the centuries for healing and technology. Many ancient cultures and civilizations built sacred sites and structures within powerful grid patterns, such as the pyramids of Egypt and the Mayan and Aztec temples. Entire cities were constructed on grids, lined up with energy fields and power spots of the Earth.

Crystal layouts are placed on or around the animal, and are used for animals that are recuperating or in recovery that are not very mobile. Stones are placed on the body for healing, and are held in place with surgical tape. They can be placed directly over the chakra points for balance, as well as energizing areas of the body and discharging toxic and stressful energies. This is often necessary to do when the animal is very relaxed and even sleeping. Stones can also be placed very close to the animal's body for similar effect.

For animals that wear them, collars can be a great place to put stones. They can be programmed with special intent for them to be healthy, happy, close to home, etc.

Grids are created in larger spaces than layouts, and actually create a holographic energy field that is multi-dimensional. They provide healing and balancing as well, but also set up fields of energy that are protective in nature, especially from E.M.F. and all forms of toxic energy. Grids can be placed on the periphery or just inside stalls, barns, pastures and corrals. They are useful underneath or in the bottom of fish tanks, cages, pens and coops. They can be set up at various points around the perimeter of large estates and ranches, or in the inside or outside corners of a home. They are excellent around sleeping areas, and if your animal sleeps on your bed, under your bed as well. When travelling in the car, they can be set on the floor or in the carrier for easier transport. And in the larger perspective, they can be buried underground at points around cities, countries and large geographical areas, programmed and placed into lakes, rivers and even oceans for healing, cleansing and blessing of the Planet.

Choosing Stones

The best stones to use for both grids and layouts are quartz crystal. I use white and rose quartz, and clear quartz. Inexpensive white and rose quartz can be found in rock quarries and landscaping supply yards, and sometimes even lapidary stores. These are the large, rough rocks, that carry powerful Earth energy that work well in large grids that require a lot of rock (when gridding your house or property, for example). Quartz is the best for programming because it easily holds the intent and stores it up to several weeks. Quartz moves energy well, and can draw in what is needed or discharge toxicity. Specific colored stones and gemstones can be added for healing and recovery, with colors that correspond to the specific chakras. For example, a cat who has been neutered can have a grid placed around his bed or under his bedding, with red or black stones (i.e. garnet or black tourmaline) to strengthen his root chakra. Pink kunzite or rose quartz could be added to soothe his heart chakra of emotional trauma from the procedure.

How Grids Work

There are two primary ways that grids work that I am aware of. Geometrically, the number of points as well as stones in the grid corresponds to the energetic field of that number. For instance, as most land animals are quadrupeds, grids using four points will be particularly attuned to them. Grids with five points, for example, can be very stabilizing and strengthening. Seven-pointed grids align the seven primary chakras and provide deep permeating healing effect. Secondly, the actual arc of energy that connects all of the stones in the grid creates a pulsating, measurable electrical field. This field is alive and in concert with the energetic field of the Earth, which also is laced with crystal veins of energy. When we create a crystal grid it bridges the planetary energetic grid with the energetic field of the animal's body, creating a hologram of tremendous healing power. The intent that is set when building the grid, whether it be for healing, protection, balance or whatever, is very important in defining and calling forth the appropriate energies.

174

Preparing the Grid

All rocks, especially quartz, are powerful energy containers and transformers. To be sure the rocks in your grid or layout are cleared and free of previous energies, soak them in salt water for 2-3 days in the sunlight. Place them in a mild salt water solution in pure water in a clear glass bowl, without designs or markings.

Once clean, select a basic grid design to place around your animal or their sleeping quarters, the house, etc. (See following page.) Place your intent into each stone by simply holding it and picturing the purpose of the grid. For example, envision all within the grid completely healed, happy, protected, etc. You can place the stone to your forehead while focusing your intent, or hold each one in your hand. Or, a grid can be set-up by using a pendulum. I point to various areas and place a stone where I get a positive answer. Often, these grids are unusual and more effective than one I would have picked. The stones should be placed on the ground or floor with the same intent, and then I take a long clear crystal point (salt water cleared) and deliberately activate the grid. I do this by drawing a line from point to point, above my head and below my feet (this is done energetically—it shouldn't be touching the other rocks), while vocally activating the grid, and invoking the power of the stones for whatever creative purpose. As rocks amplify, it is *essential* to be sure your intent is pure when programming the grid. If you feel sick or emotionally or mentally off, wait! Otherwise, you could be setting up a grid to amplify these unwanted energies.

Once grids are set up, you can add essences to each point by dropping a few drops on the rocks, placing a small bowl or glass of water near the stones, or the essence bottles themselves. For instance, when creating a grid for protection, pennyroyal or yarrow essence will help to amplify this intention and bring in the support of the devic realm to further enhance its energy.

It can be obvious when a grid needs to be cleaned—it will feel "full" and less potent. When that happens, consciously deactivate the grid, and salt water clean the stones once again.

BASIC GRID DESIGNS

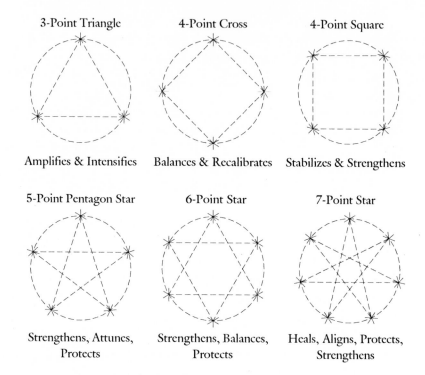

In general, stones pointed outward in a grid will discharge negative energy stored in the bodies of the animal inside the grid. Stones pointed inward will draw healing, strengthening energies in toward the animal. Animals instinctively know how to both pull in and discharge energy from their bodies. Grids make this all the more easy for them.

Magnetic and Far Infrared Healing

"The magnet . . . not only undeniably attracts steel and iron, but has also the same power over the matter of all diseases in the whole body of humanity."

—Paracelsus

Magnetic force is within the Earth and a key part of her life force. Certain areas of the Planet hold intense magnetism. These "power points" as they are sometimes called, such as Sedona, Arizona; Mount Shasta, California; many areas of the Himalayas; and the Hawaiian Islands, are but a few. People have been visiting these hot spots since early civilization for recuperation and renewal. Animals instinctively live near or visit these areas for balance and healing.

Electrical impulses are present in all substances and in the bodies of all living things. These impulses are affected greatly by magnetic force. The health of the brain and nervous system, as well as the entire body is very dependent upon this stimuli. Recent scientific research has shown that magnetic energy has very much to do with cell formation and activation, and many species of animals (many birds, fish, aquatic creatures and insects) have magnetite in their brains, which most probably holds the key to their navigational ability.

Magnetic force can be found in many rocks, and people throughout time have used these naturally occurring magnets. Since ancient times, Chinese healers have based their healing on the balance between male and female energies in the body. The ancient Greeks, who invented the word magnet, found that magnetic properties greatly relieved pain. The Romans actually used electric eels in their application of magnetics. The magnetic compass was developed from lodestone, a naturally magnetized mineral. Paracelsus understood the magnetism of all living things, and his research and discoveries helped to bring magnetic healing into the next era. Magnets are now more common in many Japanese households than aspirin. In many Asian countries, particularly Japan, therapeutic magnets are licensed as medical devices. We in the United States are just beginning to discover their healing virtues.

There are two types of magnetic therapy being used today. The pulsating direct current, where the body is placed between the positive and negative charges and the current is run through it, can be very effective for pain treatment and healing of tissue, and many other applications. However, this chapter will deal primarily with static or permanent magnets, which hold their charge permanently. They are portable, easy to use and relatively inexpensive.

Magnetic fields radiate from all living things. When there is illness, injury or less than optimal health in an animal, the magnetic field in specific areas and sometimes overall, becomes weak. Immune system compromise from the bombardment of electromagnetic frequency can be greatly relieved with magnets. Magnetic devices can provide the stimulus and presence of this energizing field. One way this occurs is by the effect the magnetized field has on the ions in the blood, increasing circulation and life force in the body. When cells become weakened by disease, their frequencies lose intensity and life-charge. When this occurs, the alternating current fields (magnetic force) lessen, resulting in poor intercellular communication and overall decline of health.

Magnets are being used primarily with horses with excellent results. They are useful for acute or chronic conditions. Race horses are experiencing increased blood flow and circulation to areas of injury, with seeming loss of pain and more mobility. Magnets have proven to assist in soft tissue repair, arthritis, joint stiffness, degenerative tissue, muscle injury, inflexible spine and joints, and toxicity and infection. Cases of bone and wound damage heal in much less time. Newest research shows that magnets can even balance the ph level, and increase hormone production and enzyme activity. There have also been improvements with emotional, mental and behavioral difficulties, such as alleviation of training and show anxiety, relief of cage, stall and kennel stress, increase of learning skills and lessening of unstable moods and behavior. With consistent magnet use, tranquilizer dosage is often able to be considerably lessened. Barking and biting have even been reduced with magnets.

Currently, there are wraps, pads, blankets, booties and individual magnets (for collars, bridles, carriers, etc.) available which can be used specifically for animals.

Far Infrared healing is a relatively new technology, which generates a specific frequency (wave length) of light from the sun. These Far Infrared waves (FIR) are the safest and most beneficial. The planet Earth, humans and animals all receive and send FIR waves, and especially when in close proximity and generating even greater heat.

Products have been developed using Infrared technology by using ceramic insulating panels and powder which generates FIR waves. Infrared saunas have been used in Asia for years, as well as in incubators in hospitals for newborns. FIR ovens have replaced microwaves in many homes as well and are finally becoming available in the U.S. In Japan, the Infrared Society is composed primarily of medical doctors and physical therapists, where they continue to research the beneficial effects of FIR waves in healing.

FIR waves have shown to alleviate skin irritations. Recovery time is shortened by increasing blood flow in the tissues. Soreness, swelling and inflammation have been reduced significantly in many cases. Research shows positive changes occur at the cellular level, stimulating enzyme activity, water conductivity and enlarging clogged capillary vessels, helping to eliminate toxins.

Infrared lamps, quilted pads and body blankets and wraps for legs and feet are available for animal healing. Finding veterinarians who are skilled with these tools may be a challenge in the United States, however magnetic and infrared therapy can be used safely and effectively on animals with a few precautions. Wraps of all types should be checked every few hours for rashes and discomfort, and should not be left on the animal for extended periods without close monitoring. Infrared lamps, as with all electrical appliances with animals, need to be used with caution and supervision.

Please see the Resources chapter for sources.

Part Four

Resources

Companies

VIBRATIONAL REMEDIES
(List of complete lines of essences by each company in Appendix B)

Alaskan Flower Essence Project
Steve Johnson
P.O. Box 1369
Homer, Alaska 99603
Phone: (907) 235-2188
Fax: (907) 235-2777
Website: www.alaskanessences.com
Email: info@alaskanessences.com
Flower essences, gem elixirs, environmental essences and combinations.

Aloha Flower Essences
Penny Medeiros
P.O. Box 2319
Kealakekua, Hawaii 96750
Phone & Fax: (808) 328-2529
Hawaiian tropical flower essences, with special combinations for animals.

Anaflora
Sharon Callahan
P.O. Box 1056
Mt. Shasta, CA 96067
Phone: (530) 926-6424
Fax: (530) 926-1245
Website: www.anaflora.com
Email: anaflora@snowcrest.net
Flower essences and sacred site essences and combinations made especially for animals. Sharon is an internationally recognized animal communication specialist. She has been making and researching flower essences for over fifteen years.

Desert Alchemy
Cynthia Athina Kemp
P.O. Box 44189
Tucson, Arizona 85733
Phone: (520) 325-1545
Fax: (520) 325-8405
Website: www.desert-alchemy.com
Email: folks@desert-alchemy.com & Workshop@desert-alchemy.com
Desert flower essences. Cynthia carries an excellent line for all female issues, which are excellent for animals. Combinations.

Flower Essence Society
Patricia Kaminski and Richard Katz
P.O. Box 459
Nevada City, California 95959
Phone: (530) 265-9163
Fax: (530) 265-6467
Excellent, extensive line of flower essences.

Green Hope Farm
Molly Sheehan
P.O. Box 125
True Road,
Meriden, New Hampshire 03770
(603) 469-3662
Email: green.hope.farm@valley.net
Wonderful variety of high quality flower essences and combinations.

Centergees Flower Essence Pharmacy
Cathy Kinnaird
48051 SE Baty Rd.
Sandy, OR 97055
VM (503) 668-7166
Fax: (503) 826-1408
Website: www.floweressences.com

Email: info@FlowerEssences.com
Supplier of essences from numerous
companies around the world.

Pegasus Products, Inc.
Fred Rubenfeld
P.O. Box 228
Boulder, CO 80306-0228
Phone: (800) 527-6104
Fax: (970) 667-3624
Website: www.pegasusproducts.com
Email: starvibe@indra.com
Flower essences, gem elixirs, starlight
elixirs and element elixirs. Combi-
nations.

ESSENTIAL OILS (AROMATHERAPY)

Clear Light
P.O. Box 551
Placitas, New Mexico 87043
Phone: (505) 867-2925
Fax: (505) 867-2925
The finest, purest and most divine
smelling cedar oil found
anywhere.

Original Swiss Aromatics
Kurt Schnaubelt
P.O. Box 6842
San Rafael, California 94903
(415) 479-9120
Entire line of excellent quality essential
oils. May be ordered directly, both
retail and wholesale.

Oshadhi
1340 G Industrial Ave.
Petaluma, California 94952
Phone: (888) 674-2344 (Toll Free)
Email: joni@oshadhiusa.com
Web: www.oshadhiusa.com
Entire line of good quality, well-priced
essential oils. May be ordered
directly, both retail and wholesale.
Entire line is sold at Whole Foods
and Wild Oats natural food stores.

Primavera Life
1157 Division St.
Napa, California 94558

(888) 588-9830 (Toll Free)
Email: primalife@aol.com
Entire line of excellent quality essential
oils. Also carry line of Demeter
oils, farmed in the Rudolph Steiner
tradition. May be ordered directly,
both retail and wholesale.

SuRos
P.O. Box 27
LaPorte, CO 80535
Phone: (970) 482-3801
Fax: (970) 472-2674
Email: lobree@frii.com
Web: www.suros.bigstep.com
Mystic Balance Revitalizing Spray is a
delightful aromatic spray with
vibrational remedies and 12
essential oils. Beautifully freshens
and clears discordant energies.
Highly recommended.

LIGHT AND COLOR DEVICES

Candles
**Crystal Journey Candles/ Crystal
Courier Imports**
451 E. 58th Ave. #1465, Box 152
Denver, Colorado 80216
Phone & Fax: (303) 296-1863
Beautiful, reasonably priced candles,
made with powerful intent.
"Angel's Influence," "Good
Health," "Harmony," "Healing"
and "Peace" are a few examples.
Very potent and effective.

Full Spectrum Lighting
American Environmental Products
Charles Botha
625 Mathew St.
Fort Collins, Colorado 80524
Phone: (970) 493-6914
Fax: (970) 482-5816
Website: www.Sunalite.com

Cutting Edge Catalog
(800) 497-9516
Website: www.cutcat.com

Tools For Exploration
9755 Independence Ave.
Chatsworth, California 91311
Phone: (800) 456-9887
Fax: (818) 407-0850
Website:
 www.toolsforexploration.com
Email:
 toolsforexploration@yahoo.com
Catalog with varied technological tools.

SOUND AND
FREQUENCY TOOLS

Inert Gas Devices
Jon Fox
P.O. Box 2209
Nevada City, California 95959
Phone: (530) 478-1002
Fax: (530) 265-0720
Website: www.hilarion.com
Email: fox@hilarion.com
Jon is a Hilarion channel who also
 makes inert gas devices.

Magnetic Devices
Magna Pak
Website: www.magnapak.com/
 pets.html
Assorted magnet line for animals.

Magnetic Force
Websites:
www.magnetic-force.com
www.therapy-magnets.com/animal/
 html
Extensive line of magnetic therapy
 especially for animals.

MagneTouch
www.magnetouch.com/product/
 prod_am.htm
Assorted magnet line for animals.

Nikken
Website:
 www.animalmagnets.bizland.com
Excellent quality magnets with a line
 especially for animals.

Pyramids
Metaforms
P.O. Box 2262
Boulder, Colorado 80306
(800) 937-4986
Fax: (303) 442-4192
Website: www.metaforms.net
Sacred geometric tools and sculptures
 for clearing and enhancing energy.
 Excellent for charging essence
 bottles.

Smog Busters
Radbusters
P.O. Box 90626
Portland, Oregon 97290-0626
Website: www.radbusters.com
Email: info@radbusters.com
Excellent line of toroids, cell phone
 tabs, and various devices to negate
 harmful electromagnetic radiation.
 Beads and tabs are excellent for
 animal collars.

SuRos
P.O. Box 27
LaPorte, CO 80535
Phone: (970) 482-3801
Fax: (970) 472-2674
Email: lobree@frii.com
Web: www.suros.bigstep.com
Makers of Lil' Buddie, purposefully
 playful while protecting from EMF,
 and the Comfort Pillow, filled with
 organic golden flax seed, herbs and
 gemstones, both encoded and
 powerful.

Tools For Exploration
9755 Independence Ave.
Chatsworth, California 91311
Phone: (800) 456-9887
Fax: (818) 407-0850
Web: www.toolsforexploration.com
Email:
 toolsforexploration@yahoo.com
Catalog with varied technological tools.

Sanctuaries & Centers

**Angel's Gate Hospice and
   Rehabilitation Center for
   Animals**
Island of Enchantment
18 Josephine Lane
Fort Salonga, NY 11768
(516) 269-7641
Email:
   enchantedconnections@MSN.com
A unique center, devoted to the multi-
faceted care and support of
critically ill animals, and animal
hospice care. A beautiful facility for
animals and education of their
human companions.

Best Friends Animal Sanctuary
Kanab, Utah
84741-5001
(801) 644-2001
Website: www.bestfriends@msn.com
One of the largest no-kill sanctuaries in
the world, housing over 1500
various animal species.

**The Elephant Sanctuary at
   Hohenwald**
P.O. Box 393
Hohenwald, Tennessee 38462
(931) 796-6500
Website: www.elephants.com
A natural habitat refuge for elephants.

W.O.L.F.
Frank and Pat Wendland
P. O. Box 1544
Laporte, Colorado 80535
(970) 416-9531
Wolf/Wolf-dog rescue & education
Excellent training and education
   facility, not taking new animals at
   this time.

W.W.W. INFO

World Wide Web Virtual Library
www.tiac.net/users/sbr/animals.html
Extensive resource for animal health,
   well-being and rights. Information
   on every animal species, with many
   links to all areas and aspects of
   animals of the world.

186

Appendix A
Suggested Music

The following list of selected music is very soothing and relaxing. My animals and I listen to it particularly for recovery and healing. The drumming CDs are a bit more vigorous, but establish pulse rhythm and heartbeat, and are very soothing and grounding for animals who are out of sorts for any reason. All of the selections listed are consistently mellow throughout, without sudden upbeat songs or passages to send any sleeping animals through the roof! I suggest low volume and candlelight (even in the daytime) for maximum effect.

CLASSICAL

Allegri, *Miserere* (Choir of St. John's College. George Guest, conductor)

Ralph Vaughan Williams:
Lark Ascending
Variations on a Theme by Thomas Tallis
Variations on Dives and Lazarus
Greensleeves Variations
Symphony No. 5 in D

NEW AGE

Patrick Bernhardt, *Atlantis Angelis*

Philip Chapman, *Higher Consciousness*

Deuter, *Garden of the Gods*

Bill Douglas, *Deep Peace*

Scott Fitzgerald, *Thunderdrums*

Paul Horn, *Peace Album*

Singh Kaur & Gary Stadler, *Fairy Nightsongs*

Robin Miller, *In the Company of Angels*

Raphael, *Music to Disappear In*
Music to Disappear In II

Steve Roach, *Dreamtime Return*

Richard Stoltzman, *Innervoices*

Eric Tingstadt, Nancy Rumbel and David Lanz, *Woodlands*

NATIVE AMERICAN

R. Carlos Nakai, *Journeys*

Joanne Shenandoah, *Life Blood*

187

Appendix B
Vibrational Remedy
Company Essence Lists

The essences listed in this book come from the companies listed below. To be absolutely sure that you have all of the current products, check with the individual companies (see Appendix A). Many are often adding new essences to their lines.

Alaskan Flower Essence Project

Flower Essences
Alder
Alpine Azalea
Angelica
Balsam Poplar
Black Spruce
Bladderwort
Blueberry Pollen
Blue Elf Viola
Bog Blueberry
Bog Rosemary
Bunchberry
Cassandra
Cattail Pollen
Chiming Bells
Columbine
Comandra
Cotton Grass
Cow Parsnip
Crowberry
Dandelion
Devil's Club

Dwarf Fireweed
False Hellebore
Fireweed
Forget-Me-Not
Foxglove
Golden Corydalis
Grass of Parnassus
Green Bells of Ireland
Green Bog Orchid
Green Fairy Orchid
Grove Sandwort
Hairy Butterwort
Harebell
Horsetail
Icelandic Poppy
Jacob's Ladder
Labrador Tea
Lace Flower
Lady's Slipper
Ladies' Tresses
Lamb's Quarters
Lavender Yarrow
Lilac
Monkshood
Moschatel

Mountain Wormwood
Nootka Lupine
Northern Lady's Slipper
Northern Twayblade
One-Sided Wintergreen
Opium Poppy
Pale Corydalis
Paper Birch
Pineapple Weed
Potato
Prickly Wild Rose
Red Elder
River Beauty
Round-Leaved Sundew
Shooting Star
Single Delight
Sitka Burnet
Sitka Spruce Pollen
Soapberry
Sphagnum Moss
Spiraea
Sticky Geranium
Sunflower
Sweetgale
Sweetgrass

188

Tamarack
Tundra Rose
Tundra Twayblade
Twinflower
White Fireweed
White Spruce
White Violet
Wild Iris
Wild Rhubarb
Wild Sweet Pea
Willow
Yarrow
Yellow Dryas

Gem Elixirs
Aquamarine
Aventurine
Azurite
Black Tourmaline
Bloodstone
Brazilian Amethyst
Brazilian Quartz
Carnelian
Chrysocolla
Chrysoprase
Citrine
Covellite
Diamond
Emerald
Fluorite
Fluorite Combo
Gold
Green Jasper
Hematite
Herkimer Diamond
Jade
Jadeite
Kunzite
Lapis Lazuli
Malachite
Moldavite
Montana Rhodochrosite
Moonstone
Opal
Orange Calcite
Pearl
Peridot
Pyrite
Rhodochrosite
Rhodolite Garnet
Rose Quartz
Ruby

Rutilated Quartz
Sapphire
Sapphire/Ruby
Scepter Amethyst
Smoky Quartz
Spectrolite
Star Sapphire
Sugalite
Tiger's Eye
Topaz
Turquoise
Watermelon Tourmaline

Environmental Essences
Chalice Well
Full Moon Reflection
Glacier River
Greenland Icecap
Liard Hot Springs
Northern Lights
Polar Ice Cap
Portage Glacier
Rainbow Glacier
Solstice Storm
Solstice Sun
Tidal Forces

Aloha Hawaiian Tropical Flower Essences

Amazon Swordplant
Avocado
Awapuhi-melemele (Yellow Ginger)
Bamboo Orchid
Bougainvillea
Chinese Violet
Coffee
Cotton
Cup of Gold
Day-Blooming Waterlily
Hau (Hibiscus)
Hinahina-ku-kahakai
Ili'ahi (Hawaiian Sandalwood)
Ilima
Impatiens
Jade Vine
Kamani
Koa (Hawaiian Acacia)

Kou
Kukui (Candlenut Tree)
La'au'-aila (Castor Bean)
Lehua
Lotus
Macadamia
Mai'a (Banana)
Mamane
Mango
Milo
Naio
Nana-honua (Angel's Trumpet)
Nani-ahiahi (Four O'Clock)
Naupaka-kahakai
Night-Blooming Waterlily
Niu (Coconut)
Noho-malie
Noni (Indian Mulberry)
Ohai Ali'i
Ohelo
Ohi'a-'ai (Mountain Apple)
Panini-awa'awa (Aloe)
Pa-nini-o-ka (Night-Blooming Cereus)
Papaya (male and female)
Passion Flower
Pa'u-o-Hi'iaka
Pleomele fragrans
Plumbago
Poha (Cape Gooseberry)
Pua-hoku-hihi (Wax Plant)
Pua-kenikeni
Pua melia (Plumeria)
Pua-pilo
Pukiawe
Spider Lily
Stenogyne Calaminthoides
Ti (or Ki)
Uala (Purple Sweet Potato)
Ulei
Water Poppy
Wiliwili

Special Blends

189

Anaflora

Flower Essences
Alpine Pussy Paws
Alpine Shooting Star
Alyssum
Amaranthus
Bear Grass
Blackberry
Blue Eyed Grass
Bleeding Heart
Broadleaf Lupine
Bunchberry
California Pitcher Plant
California Poppy
California Wild Rose
Castle Lake Azalea
Cat's Ears
Chamomile
Chaparral Iris
Checker Mallow
Chicory
Chinese Wisteria
Clematis
Comfrey
Coral Root
Cosmos
Cow Parsnip
Coyote Mint
Daffodil
Dandelion
Deerbrush
Delphinium (Larkspur)
Dogwood
Douglas Iris
Douglas Violet
Dwarf Mountain
 Manzanita
Dwarf Purple Monkey-
 flower
Evening Primrose
False Hellebore
Farewell to Spring
Fennel
Forget-Me-Not
Foxglove
Fragrant Water Lily
French Marigold
Fuschia
Gold Plate
Grape Hyacinth
Heart Leaved Bittercress

Heart's Ease
Holly
Hooded Lady's Tresses
Hyssop
Indian Pond Lily
Iris Versicolor
Lady's Slipper
Lavender
Lilac
Live Forever
Lobelia
Mallow
Manzanita
Marsh Marigold
Miniature Lupine
Monk's Hood
Morning Glory
Mountain Fleabane
Mullein
Mustard
Onion
Oregon Grape
Pearly Everlasting
Peony
Periwinkle
Pine
Pine Violet
Pink Milkweed
Pink Monkey Flower
Plantain
Pride of the Mountain
Purple Crocus
Quaking Grass
Queen Anne's Lace
Rabbit Brush
Red Clover
Scarlet Paintbrush
Scotch Broom
Self Heal
Shasta Alpine Aster
Shasta Daisy
Shasta Lily
Shasta Star Flower
Shasta Star Tulip
Shasta White Lupine
Shasta White Sage
Shooting Star
Siskiyou Iris
Small Tiger Lily
Snapdragon
Squash
St. John's Wort

Sunflower
Sweet Briar
Sweet Pea
Thimbleberry
Tiger Lily
Tofield's Swamp Lily
Twinflower
Wagon Creek Buttercup
Water Cress
Water Hemlock
Western Choke Cherry
White Clover
White Crocus
White Yarrow
Wild Ginger
Wild Strawberry
Wisteria
Yellow Monkey Flower
Yerba Santa

Rock Waters
Big Springs Rock Water
Panther Spring Rock
 Water
Squaw Spring Rock
 Water

Desert Alchemy

Agave
Aloe
Arizona Sycamore
Arizona White Oak
Arroyo Willow
Bear Grass
Big Root Jatropha
Bisbee Beehive Cactus
Black Locust
Bloodroot
Bougainvillea
Bouvardia
Buffalo Gourd
Camphorweed
Candy Barrel Cactus
Cane Cholla
Canyon Grapevine
Cardinal Flower
Cardon
Chaparral
Claret Cup Hedgehog
Cliff Rose
Compass Barrel Cactus

Coral Bean
Cow Parsnip
Crownbeard
Crown of Thorns
Damiana
Desert Bloom
Desert Christmas Cholla
Desert Holly
Desert Marigold
Desert Sumac
Desert Willow
Devil's Claw
Dogbane
Dyssodia
Ephedra
Evening Star
Fairy Duster
Fire Prickly Pear Cactus
Fishhook Cactus
Foothills Paloverde
Hackberry
Hairy Larkspur
Hedgehog Cactus
Hoptree
Indian Root
Indian Tobacco
Indigo Bush
Inmortal
Jojoba
Jumping Cholla Cactus
Klein's Pencil Cholla
    Cactus
Lavender Wand
    Penstemon
Lilac
Mala Mujer
Mariola
Mariposa Lily
Melon Loco
Mesquite
Mexican Shell Flower
Mexican Star
Milky Nipple Cactus
Morning Glory Tree
Mountain Mahogany
Mullein
Ocotillo
Oregon Grape
Organ Pipe Cactus
Palmer Amaranth
Pencil Cholla Cactus
Periwinkle

Pink Pond Lily
Pomegranate
Prickly Pear Cactus
Prickle Poppy
Purple Aster
Purple Mat
Queen of the Night
    Cactus
Rainbow Cactus
Ratany
Red Root
Red Orange Epiphyllum
Sacred Datura
Saguaro Cactus
Salsify
Sangra de Drago
Scarlet Morning Glory
Scorpion Weed
Senita Cactus
Silverleaf Nightshade
Smartweed
Soaptree Yucca
Sow Thistle
Spanish Bayonet Yucca
Spineless Prickly Pear
Staghorn Cholla Cactus
Star Leaf
Star Primrose
Strawberry Cactus
Syrian Rue
Tarbush
Teddy Bear Cholla
    Cactus
Theresa Cactus
Thistle
Thurber's Gilia
Violet Curls
Violet Soldier
White Desert Primrose
White Desert Zinnia
White Evening Primrose
Whitethorn
Wild Buckwheat
Windflower
Wolfberry
Woven Spine Pineapple
    Cactus
Zephyr Lily

Special Formulas

Flower Essence Society

Acacia
Agrimony
Alfalfa
Almond
Aloe Vera
Alpine Aster
Alpine Lily
Angel's Trumpet
Angelica
Apple
Apricot
Arnica
Aspen
Aster
Avocado
Baby Blue Eyes
Banana
Basil
Bearded Protea
Bedstraw
Bee Balm
Beech
Birch
Bistort
Black Cohosh
Blackberry
Black-Eyed Susan
Blackthorn
Bleeding Heart
Bloodroot
Borage
Broccoli
Burdock
Buttercup
Calendula
California Fuchsia
California Pitcher Plant
California Poppy
California White Rose
California Wild Rose
Calla Lily
Canyon Dudleya
Carob
Catchfly
Cayenne
Cedar
Centaury
Cerato
Chamomile

Chaparral
Cherry
Cherry Plum
Chestnut Bud
Chicory
Cholla
Christmas Rose
Chrysanthemum
Cinquefoil
Clarkia
Cleavers
Clematis
Coffee
Coltsfoot
Columbine
Comfrey
Coral Root
Coreopsis
Corn
Corn Lily
Cosmos
Crab Apple
Cranesbill
Daffodil
Dandelion
Daphne
Deerbrush
Dill
Dogwood
Dutchman's Breeches
Easter Lily
Echinacea
Edelweiss
Elm
Eucalyptus
Evening Primrose
Fairy Lantern
Fawn Lily
Feverfew
Fig
Filaree
Fireweed
Five-Flower Formula
Forget-Me-Not
Forsythia
Four-Leaf Clover
Foxglove
Fuchsia
Garlic
Gentian
Gilia
Ginger

Golden Ear Drops
Golden Ragwort
Goldenrod
Goldenrod Bud
Golden Yarrow
Gorse
Grapefruit
Gum-Plant
Harvest Brodiaea
Hawthorn
Heather
Hibiscus
Holly
Hollyhock
Honeysuckle
Hopi Dye Amaranth
Hops
Hornbeam
Hound's Tongue
Hyssop
Impatiens
Indian Paintbrush
Indian Pink
Iris
Ironweed
Jasmine
Jewel Flower
Kale
Lady's Mantle
Lady's Purse
Lady's Slipper
Lamb's Ears
Larch
Larkspur
Lavender
Lavender, French
Lemon
Lilac
Lion's Tail
Liverwort
Loofa
Loquat
Lotus
Love-Lies-Bleeding
Madia
Madrone
Mallow
Manzanita
Marigold
Mariposa Lily
Milkweed
Mimulus

Mistletoe
Monkshood
Morning Glory
Mountain Pennyroyal
Mountain Pride
Mugwort
Mullein
Mustard
Namaqualand Daisy
Nasturtium
Nectarine
Nicotiana
Noni
Oak
Oconee Bells
Oleander
Olive
Onion
Orange
Oregon Grape
Pansy
Papaya
Passion Flower
Peach
Pear
Pennyroyal
Penstemon
Peppermint
Persimmon
Petunia
Pine
Pink Monkeyflower
Pink Yarrow
Plantain
Plum
Poison Oak
Pomegranate
Porcupine Cactus
Prickly Pear Cactus
Pretty Face
Purple Monkeyflower
Pussy Paws
Quaking Grass
Queen Anne's Lace
Quince
Rabbitbrush
Ragweed
Red Bud
Red Chestnut
Red Clover
Red Larkspur
Redwood

Rock Rose
Rock Water
Rosemary
Rue
Sage
Sagebrush
Saguaro
Saint John's Wort
Scarlet Monkeyflower
Scarlet Pimpernel
Scleranthus
Scotch Broom
Self-Heal
Sequoia
Shasta Daisy
Shasta Lily
Shining Flower
Shooting Star
Sierra Iris
Snapdragon
Soap Plant
Sonoma Sage
Speedwell
Spice Bush
Spikenard, California
Spreading Phlox
Squash (Acorn)
Squash (Crookneck)
Squash (Zucchini)
Star of Bethlehem
Star Thistle
Star Tulip
Sticky Monkeyflower
Squaw Currant
Star Jasmine
Stickseed
Stinging Nettle
Strawberry
Sulphur Flower
Sunflower
Sweet Alyssum
Sweet Chestnut
Sweet Pea
Tansy
Thyme
Tiger Lily
Ti Plant
Trillure
Trumpet Vine
Turk's Cap
Turnip
Valerian

Vervain
Vine
Violet
Wallflower
Walnut
Watermelon
Water Violet
White Chestnut
White Clover
Wild Oat
Wild Rose
Willow
Wisteria
Witch Hazel
Wood Betony
Yampa
Yarrow
Yarrow, Yellow
Yarrow Special Formula
Yellow Star Tulip
Yerba Santa
Zinnia

Special Combinations

Green Hope Farm

Agrippina Rose
Alex Mackenzie Rose
Allamanda
Aloe Ciliaris
Aloe, Coral
Aloe Species
Aloe Vera
Amaryllis
Andalisa
Angelica
Anthurium
Arrowhead
Asclepias
Avocado
Baby Blue Eyes
Banana
Bells of Ireland
Bermudiana
Bignonia
Bird of Paradise
Blackberry
Black Currant
Black Ebony
Black Eyed Susan
Bloodroot

Blue Flag Iris
Boneset
Borage
Bottlebrush
Bottle Gentian
Bottle Palm
Broccoli
Cabbage
Calendula
California Poppy
Calla Lily
Calliandra
Calophyllum
Capeweed
Cardinal Flower
Carouby de Maussane
  Pea
Cedar
Century Plant
Chamomile
Chicory
Chinese Fan Palm
Chinese Hat Plant
Chives
Clematis
Clitoria
Clivia
Cochineal Cactus
Coconut Palm
Coltsfoot
Comfrey
Coralita
Coral Pink Rose
Corn
Cosmos
Cotton
Crab Apple
Cucumber
Daffodil
Dandelion
Date Palm
Datura, Moonlight
Datura, Sunlight
Delphinium
Devil's Bit Scabiosa
Dombeya Wallwachii
Dracaena
Easter Lily Vine
Echinacea
Eggplant
Epimedium
Eryngium

193

European Fan Palm
Eyebright
Eyes of Mary
Fairy Rose
Feverfew
Figi Fan Palm
Fireweed
Fishtail Palm
Fleabane
Foamflower
Frangipani
Freesia
French Marigold
Gall of the Earth
Gardenia
Ginger
Golden Areca Palm
Goldenrod
Golden Showers
Graniana Rose
Grapefruit
Gruss An Aachen Rose
Hardhack
Harebell from the
  Burren
Hawthorn
Heavenly Bamboo
Henry Hudson Rose
Honeybees in the White
  Hawthorn
Honeysuckle
Hoya Purpurea Fusca
Hyssop
Ice Plant
Indian Paintbrush/
  Orange Hawkweed
Indian Pipe
Irish Heath
Ixora
Jade
Jamaica Dogwood
Jasmine
Jatropha
Jewelweed
Joe Pye Weed
Justicia Carnea
La Belle Sultane Rose
Lady Palm
Larkspur
Lauriana Rose
Lavender
Lemon

Lilac
Lily of the Valley
Lime
Locust & Wild Honey
Logan's Force of Truth
Loquat
Lungwort
Magnolia
Mallow
Maltese Cross
Maple
Marsh Orchid from the
  Burren
Mary Queen of Scots
  Rose
Mary Rose
Meadow Rue
Meadow Sweet
Mignonette
Milkweed
Mimosa
Monkey Tail
Morning Glory
Mustard
Mutabilis Rose
Mystery Palm
Nasturtium
Niella
Old Blush China Rose
Olivewood
Orange
Orange Hawkweed
Painkiller Plant
Pale Pink Rose
Pandorea
Papaya
Partridgeberry
Passion Flower
Peace Lily
Pear
Pennyroyal
Petunia St. Germain
Pink Baby's Breath
Pink Lady's Slipper
Pink Laurel
Pink Tecoma
Pink Yarrow from the
  Cliffs of Moher
Pomegranate
Potato Vine
Precious Blood
Prickly Pear

Pumpkin
Pyrola Elliptica
Queen Anne's Lace
Queen Palm
Radish
Ragwort
Rain of Gold
Red Clover
Red Hibiscus
Red Mangrove
Red Rugosa Rose
Rhubarb
Rosa Banksia
Rosa Mundi
Rose a Parfum de l'Hay
Rose Apple
Rosemary
Royal Ponciana
Ruby Gold Orchid
Sage
Sago Palm
Scarlet Runner Bean
Sceptre of Power Flower
Screw Pine
Scullcap
Self Heal
Shrimp Plant
Simonetta
Small Woodland Orchid
Snapdragon
Solandra
Spanish Bayonet
Spice Tree
Spider Lily
Spiderwort
Star Flower
Star of Bethlehem
St. John's Wort
Summer Snowflake
Sunflower
Swamp Candles
Sweet Pea
Sweet William
Temple Cloud Orchid
Thistle
Thyme
Titan
Tomato
Tree Peony
Trillium
Trout Lily
True Wood Sorrel

Turnera
Vanda Orchid
Vanda Rothschildiana
Vetch
Violet Sweet Pea
Violet T. F. Violet
Vitex
Water Hyacinth
White Bleeding Heart
White California Poppy
White Cedar
White Hibiscus
White Lady's Slipper
White Mullein
White Nicotiana
White Trillium
White Yarrow
Wild Columbine
Wild Iris
Wild Oats
Wild Strawberry
Wild Thrift
Wild Wood Violet
Wintergreen
Wood Sage from the
  Burren
Yellow Mullein
Yellow Water Lily
Zinnia
Zucchini

Special Combinations

Pegasus Products

Flower Essences
Acacia
Aconite
Agave Yaquiana
Agrimony
Allamanda
Allspice
Almond
Aloe Eru
Aloe Vera
Alyogyne Huegelli
Amaranthus-Golden
Amaranthus-Red
Amaryllis
Angelica
Angel's Trumpet
Apple

Apricot
Arnica Mollis
Artichoke
Asparagus
Aspen
Aster-Pink
Astrophytum
Avocado
Bachelor's Button
Balm-Lemon
Balm of Gilead
Bamboo-Sacred
Banana
Banksia Baxtena
Banksia Laricina
Banksia Marginata
Banyan Tree
Barley
Basil-Sacred
Basil-Sweet
Bayberry
Bear Grass
Beauty Secret
Bedstraw
Bee Balm
Beech
Belinda Rose
Belladonna
Bells of Ireland
Birch-Female
Birch-Male
Birch-Male/Female
Bird of Paradise
Bistort
Bittersweet
Blackberry
Blazing Star
Bleeding Heart
Blessed Thistle
Bloodroot
Blue Flag
Blue Witch
Borage
Bo Tree
Bottlebrush
Bougainvillea
Brazil Nut
Breadfruit
Brittlebrush
Brussel Sprouts
Buff Beauty
Bugbane

Burdock
Buttercup
Butterfly Lily
Cabbage
Cacao
Calendula
California Bay Laurel
California Buckeye
California Pitcher Plant
California Poppy
Calla Lily
Calothamnus Validus
Calypso Orchid
Camphor
Cantaloupe
Cape Honeysuckle
Carnation
Carob
Carrot
Cashew Nut Tree
Castilian Rose
Castor Bean Tree
Caterpillar Plant
Catnip
Cat's Tail
Cayenne
Cedar
Celandine
Celosia
Centaury
Century Agave
Cerato
Cereus Cactus
Chamomile-Dye
Chamomile-German
Chamomile-Wild
Chaparral
Chaulmoogra
  Hydnocarpus
Cherry Plum
Cherry-Sweet
Chervil
Chestnut Bud-White
Chestnut Flower-White
Chestnut-Red
Chestnut-Sweet
Chickweed
Chicory
Chin Cactus
Choke Cherry
Chrysanthemum
Cinnamon Tree

Cinquefoil
Clarkia
Clematis
Clover-Red
Clove Tree
Coconut Tree
Coffee
Cohosh-Black
Colchicum
Coleus
Coltsfoot
Columbine
Comfrey
Coralroot
Coralroot-Spotted
Coriander
Corn-Hopi
Corn-Sweet
Cosmos
Cotton
Crab Apple
Crape Myrtle
Creeping Thistle
Crown of Thorns
Curry Leaf Tree
Cyclamen
Daffodil
Dahlia
Daisy-English
Daisy-Shasta
Dandelion
Daphne
Date Palm
Datura Sanguinea
Dayflower
Deer's Tongue
Desert Barrel Cactus
Dill
Dog Rose
Dogwood
Dragon Flower Cactus
Dutchman's Breeches
Easter Lily
Easter Lily Cactus
Echinacea
Edelweiss
Elecampagne
Elephant's Head
Elm-English
Endive
Eucalyptus
Everlasting

Eyebright
Fennel
Ferocactus
Fever few
Figwort
Fireweed
Flame of the Forest
Flamingo Lily
Flax
Floss Flower
Forget-Me Not
Four Leaf Clover
Foxglove
Frangipani
Fuschia
Gardenia
Garlic
Garlic-Chives
Gentian
Geranium
Germander
Gilia-Scarlet
Ginger-Red
Ginger-Wild
Ginseng
Gladiola
Goldenrod
Goldenseal
Gooseberry
Gorse
Gotu Kola
Grapefruit
Green Rein Orchid
Green Rose
Gum Plant
Hardenbergia
   Comptonia
Harvest Brodiaea
Hawthorne-English
Heather
Heliconia
Helleborus-Black
Henbane
Henna
Hibiscus
Holly
Hollyhock
Holy Thorn
Honeysuckle
Hooded Ladies Tresses
Hops
Horehound

Horseradish
Horsetail
Hound's Tongue
Hyacinth
Hydrangea-Green
Hyssop
Impatiens
Indian Paintbrush
Indian Pink
Ipecac
Iris-Sierra
Jacob's Ladder
Jasmine
Jerusalem Artichoke
Jimson Weed
Jojoba
Jungle Flame Flower
Khat
Kidney Bean
Kinnick-Kinnick
Kiwi
Koenign van Daenmark
Kohlrabi
Ladies Purse
Lady's Mantle
Lantana
Larkspur
Lavender
Lavender-English
Lavender-French
Lemon
Lemmon's Paintbrush
Leopard Lily
Lettuce
Licorice
Lilac
Lily of the Valley
Lima Bean
Lime
Lion's Tail
Litchi
Live Forever
Lobelia
Lobivia Cactus
Loosestrife
Loquat
Lotus
Love in a Mist
Luffa
Lungwort
Macadamia
Macartney Rose

Madia
Magnolia
Mahogany
Mallow
Mandrake
Mango
Manzanita
Maple
Marigold-French
Marjoram
Meadowsweet
Melaleuca
Mesquite
Mezereum
Milkmaids
Milk Thistle
Milkweed
Millet
Mimulus
Mistletoe
Mock Orange
Moneyplant
Monkeyflower
Monkshood
Monvillea Cactus
Morning Glory
Motherwort
Mountain Laurel
Mountain Misery
Mountain Pride
Mugwort
Mulberry-Red
Mullein
Mushroom
Mustard
Myrtlewood Tree
Nasturtium
Nectarine
Neoporteria Cactus
Noble Star Cactus
Nutmeg
Oak-English
Ohi'a Lehua
Okra
Old Maid
Old Woman of the
    Mountain
Oleander
Olive
Onion
Orange

Orange Flame Flower
    Cactus
Orchid
Orchid Combo-Tahiti
Orchid Tree
Oregon Grape Root
Owl's Clover
Pampas Grass
Pansy
Papaya
Papyrus
Parsley
Pasque Flower
Passion Flower
Peach
Peanut
Pear
Pecan
Pegasus Orchid Cactus
Pennyroyal
Pennyroyal-Mountain
Penstemon
Peony
Pepper
Peppermint
Perilla
Periwinkle
Persimmons- Female
Persimmons-Male
Persimmons-Male/
    Female
Petunia
Phlox
Phytolacca Diocia
Pimpernel-Scarlet
Pineapple
Pineapple-Guava
Pinedrops
Pine-Monterey
Pine-Scotch
Pink Powder Puff
Pistachio
Pitcher Plant
Plantain-Psyllium
Pleurisy Root
Plumeria
Plum Tree
Poinsettia
Poison Ivy
Poke Weed
Pomegranate
Potato

Pot of Gold
Prayer Plant
Prickly Pear Cactus
Prickly Poppy
Protea-Pink Mink
Pumpkin-Female
Pumpkin-Male
Pumpkin-Male/Female
Purple Nightshade
Pussy's Paw
Pyrethrum
Quaking Grass
Queen Anne's Lace
Quinoa
Rabbitbrush
Radish
Ragweed-Ambrosia
Raspberry
Rattail Cactus
Rattlesnake Plantain
    Orchid
Red Bud-Judas Tree
Red Mountain Heather
Redwood
Rhododendron
Rhubarb
Rice
Robinia
Rock Rose
Rock Rose Cistus
Rosa Banksiae Lutescens
Rosa Beauty Secret
Rosa Beggeriana
Rosa Buff Beauty
Rosa Californica
Rosa Campion
Rosa Centifolia Cristata
Rosa Chinesis Mutabilis
Rosa Cinnamonea
Rosa Corifolia Froebelii
Rosa Corymbifera
Rosa Damascena Bifera
Rosa Damascena
    Versicolor
Rosa Escae
Rosa Farreri Persetosa
Rosa Fendleri Woodsii
Rosa Foetida Bicolor
Rosa Gallica Officinalis
Rosa Gallica Versicolor
Rosa Hardii
Rosa Hemisphaerica

Rosa Honorine de
  Brabant
Rosa Horrida
Rosa Hugonis
Rosa Kamtchatica
Rosa Longicuspis
Rosa Macrantha
Rosa Macrophylla
Rosa Nutkana
Rosa Odorata
Rosa Poppy
Rosa Roxburghii
Rosa Rubrifolia
Rosa Rugosa Alba
Rosa Sericea
Rosa Sinowilsonii
Rosa Villosa
Rosa Virginia
Rosa Webbiana
Rosa Xanthina
Rosemary
Rose of Sharon
Rubber Tree
Rue
Rye
Sage
Sagebrush
Saguaro
St. John's Wort
Sandalwood
Sassafras
Scarlet Mimulus
Scarlet Runner Bean
Scleranthus Annus
Scotch Broom
Sea Lettuce
Self Heal
Sensitive Plant
Shasta Lily
Shepherd's Purse
Shooting Star
Shrimp Plant
Sierra Rein Orchid
Silk Tree
Silversword
Skullcap
Snapdragon
Snowplant
Soaproot
Solomon's Seal
Sorrel
Sourgrass

Spice Bush
Spider Lily(Red)
Spiderwort
Spikenard
Spring Beauty
Spruce
Squash-Acorn-Female
Squash-Acorn-F/M
Squash-Acorn-Male
Squash-Crookneck-
  Female
Squash-Crookneck-F/M
Squash-Crookneck-Male
Squash-Zucchini-Female
Squash-Zucchini-F/M
Squash-Zucchini-Male
Squaw Vine
Starflower
Star Jasmine
Star of Bethlehem
Star Thistle
Star Tulip
Stephanotis
Stinging Nettle
Stoneroot
Strawberry
Sugar Beet
Sugar Cane
Sulcorebutia Cactus
Sun Cup
Sunflower
Swamp Onion
Sweet Alyssum
Sweet Flag
Sweet Pea
Sycamore
Tague
Tamarind
Tansy
Tarragon-French
Tea Plant
Tea Tree
Thyme
Tiare
Tiger Lily
Tobacco
Tomato
Tree of Life
Tree Opuntia
Tree Tobacco
Trillium-Red
Trumpet Vine

Tuberose
Tulip
Turk's Cap
Valerian
Vanilla
Venus Fly Trap
Vervain
Viburnum
Vine
Waikiki Rainbow Cactus
Wake Robin
Wallflower
Walnut-English
Washington Lily
Watermelon-Female
Watermelon-Female/
  Male
Watermelon-Male
Water Violet
Wheat
Willow-Weeping
Wintergreen
Wisteria-Chinese
Witch Hazel
Wood Betony
Woodruff-Sweet
Wooly Sunflower
Wormwood
Yarrow-Pink
Yarrow-Red
Yarrow-White
Yarrow-Yellow
Yerba Buena
Yerba Mate
Yerba Santa
Ylang Ylang
Yucca
Zinnia

Gem Elixirs
Abalone
Acharandite
Adamite
Aegerine
Agate-Blue Lace
Agate-Botswana
Agate-Carnelian
Agate-Fire
Agate-Moss
Agate-Picture
Albite
Alexandrite

Alunite
Amazonite
Amber
Amblygonite
Amethyst
Anapoite
Anatase
Anhydrite
Anglesite
Annabergite
Antimony
Antlerite
Apatite
Apophyllite
Aquamarine
Aragonite
Arthurite
Artinite
Asphalt
Astrophyllite
Atacamite
Augite
Autunite
Aventurine
Azeztulite
Azurite
Azurite-Malachite
Barite
Benitoite
Berthierite
Beryl
Beryllonite
Beryl-Red
Beudantite
Bismuth
Bloodstone
Bog-Peat
Boji Stone
Boleite
Boracite
Brass
Brazilianite
Brochantite
Broshentite
Bronze
Brucite
Cacoxenite
Calamine
Calcite
Caledonite
Callaghanite
Carbon Steel

Carletonite
Cassiterite
Cavanisite
Celestite
Cerussite
Chabazite
Chalcedony
Charoite
Chenevixite
Childrenite
Chorlesite
Chrome Diopside
Chromium
Chrysoberyl
Chrysocolla
Chrysolite
Chrysoprase
Cinnabar
Clay
Clinoclase
Clinoptilolite
Coal
Cobaltian Calcite
Cobaltian Dolomite
Cobaltite
Colemantite
Columbite
Conichalcite
Copper
Coral-Black
Coral-Blue
Coral-Pink
Coral-Purple
Coral-Red
Coral-Red/White
Coral-White
Coral-Yellow
Cordierite
Cornetite
Covellite
Crandallite
Cream of Tartar
Creedite
Cristobalite
Crocoite
Cuprite
Cuprosklodowskite
Cyanotrichite
Danburite
Datolite
Descloizite
Diaboleite

Diaspore
Dioptase
Diamond-Black
Diamond-Blue
Diamond-Gray
Diamond-Green
Diamond-Orange
Diamond-Pink
Diamond-Red
Diamond-White
Diamond-Yellow
Diopside
Dioptase
Duftite
Dumortierite
Durangite
Dussertite
Eilat Stone
Electrum
Emerald
Enargite
Endlichite
Enstatite
Enstatite-Cat's Eye
Eosphorite
Epistilbite
Erythrite
Ettringite
Euclase
Eudialyte
Faustite
Feldspar
Ferberite
Ferro-Axinite
Flint
Fluorite
Franckeite
Fuchsite
Galena
Gallium
Garnet-Hessonite
Garnet-Rhodolite
Garnet-Spessartine
Garnet-Tsavorite
Garnet-Uvarovite
Garnierite
Gaspeite
Gearksutite
Gem Silica
Glass-Fulganite
Glaucocerinite
Gold

199

Gordonite
Gormanite
Goshenite
Granite
Graphite
Gypsum
Gyrolite
Halite (Salt)
Halloysite
Hancockite
Hematite
Hemimorphite
Herderite
Herkimer Diamond
Heulandite
Hiddenite
Huebnerite
Inderite
Inesite
Iridium
Ivory
Jade
Jade-Black
Jade-Lavender
Jadeite
Jamesonite
Jarosite
Jasper- Idar Oberstein
Jasper-Green
Jasper-Picture
Jasper-Red
Jasper-Yellow
Jet
Kaemmererite
Kasolite
Kermesite
Kinoite
Krupkaite
Kunzite
Kunzite-Cat's Eye
Kutnahorite
Kyanite
Labradorite
Labradorite Spectrolite
Lapis Lazuli
Larimar
Laumontite
Lava
Lavendulan
Lazulite
Lazurite
Lead

Lepidocrocite
Lepidolite
Libethenite
Limestone
Linarite
Lirconite
Lodestone (Neg)
Lodestone (Neg/Pos)
Lodestone (Pos)
Ludlamite
Magnesite
Magnesium
Magnetite (Neg)
Magnetite (Neg/Pos)
Magnetite (Pos)
Malachite
Manganese
Manganocalcite
Marble
Margarite
Mesolite-Pink
Metaschoderite
Meteorite
Milarite
Millbillillie
Mimetite
Mixite
Moldavite
Molybdenum
Moonstone
Moonstone-Cat's Eye
Morganite
Mother of Pearl (Oyster
    Shell)
Muscovite
Natrolite
Nephrite
Neptunite
Northuptite
Obsidian
Okenite
Onyx
Opal-Blue
Opal-Cherry
Opal-Dark
Opal-Fire
Opal-Jelly
Opal-Light
Orthoclase
Osarizawaite
Palladium
Papagoite

Pearl (Black)
Pearl (Dark)
Pearl (Dark/Light)
Pearl (Light)
Percylite
Peridot
Petrified Wood
Phenakite
Philipsburgite
Pistacite
Plancheite
Platinum
Porphyry
Portlandite
Powellite
Prehenite
Purpurite
Pyragyrite
Pyrite
Pyrolusite
Pyromorphite
Pyrophylite
Pyroxmangite
Quartz-Black (Smoky)
Quartz-Blue
Quartz-Citrine (Yellow)
Quartz-Dendritic
Quartz-Green
Quartz-Lepidocrocite-
    Goethite
Quartz-Lepidocrocite
    Hematite
Quartz-Rose
Quartz-Rutilated
Quartz-Solution
Quartz-Tourmaline
Quartz-White
Quartzite
Ramsdellite
Realgar
Rhodizite
Rhodochrosite
Rhodonite
Rhyolite (Wonderstone)
Rosasite
Rubellite
Ruby
Rutile
Sand
Sandstone
Sapphire-Blue
Sapphire-Green

Sapphire-Orange
Sapphire-Pink
Sapphire-Purple
Sapphire-Yellow
Sarabauite
Sard
Sardonyx
Scapolite-Purple
Scarab
Scheelite
Scholzite
Scolecite
Scorodite
Selenite
Sepiolite
Serandite
Seraphinite
Serpentine
Shattuckite
Siderite
Silver
Smithsonite
Soapstone
Sodalite
Spangolite
Sphalerite
Sphene
Spinel
Spurrite
Star Diopside
Star Garnet
Star Moonstone
Star Quartz-Rose
Star Quartz-White
Star Ruby
Star Sapphire
Staurolite
Stellerite
Stibnite
Strombolite
Strontianite
Sugilite (Royal Azel)
Sulfur
Sunstone
Szenicsite
Talc
Tanzanite-Blue
Tanzanite-Green
Tarnowitzite
Tektite
Tellurium
Tennantite

Tetrahedrite
Thomsonite
Thulite
Tiger's Eye
Tin
Titanium
Topaz-Blue
Topaz-Yellow
Torbernite
Tourmaline-Black
    (Schorl)
Tourmaline-Blue
    (Indicolite)
Tourmaline-Cat's Eye
Tourmaline-Chrome
Tourmaline-Green
Tourmaline-Opalized
Tourmaline-Paraiba
Tourmaline-Quartz
Tourmaline-Watermelon
Tourmaline-White
    (Uvite)
Tremolite
Trinityite
Tuffa
Tunnelite
Turquoise
Tyrolite
Ulexite
Ussingite
Vanadinite
Variscite
Vauxite
Vesuvianite
Veszelyite
Villaumite
Vivianite
Wavelite
Wiggleite
Willemite
Woodwardite
Wulfenite
Wurtzite
Xonotlite
Yttrotungstite
Zinc
Zincite
Zircon
Zoisite
Zunyite

Starlight Elixirs
Adhara
Alcyone
Aldebaran
Alderamin
Algenib
Algieba
Algol
Alhena
Alioth
Alkaid
Alludra
Almach
Al Nasl
Alnilam
Alnitak
Alphard
Alphecca
Alpheratz
Alrisha
Altair
Andromeda Galaxy
Antares
Arcturus
Arneb
Ascella
Asellus Australis
Asellus Borealis
Bellatrix
Beta Corvii
Betelgeuse
Capella
Caph
Castor
Cheleb
Cor Caroli
Cursa
Dabih
Delta Cygni
Delta Ophiuchi
Deneb
Deneb Algedi
Denebola
Diphda
Dscubba
Dubhe
Dumbell Nebula M27
Electra (Pleiades)
El Nath
El Tarf
Enif
Epsilon Leonis

Epsilon Perseii
Fomalhaut
Gamma Persei
Gamma Piscium
Gertab
Giedi
Gienah
Gomeisa
Graffias
Hale-Bopp Comet
Hamal
Han
H & Chi Persei
Helios (The Sun)
Hyades
Iota Aurigae
Iota Orionis
Izar
Jupiter
Kaus Australis
Kaus Borealis
Kochab
Kornephoros
Lesath
Luna (The Moon)
M1 (Crab Nebula)
M2
M3 (Globular Cluster)
M5
M6
M7
M8 (Lagoon Nebula)
M10
Mll
M12
M13 (Hercules Cluster)
M15
M20 (Trifid Nebula)
M22
M23
M27 (Dumbell Nebula)
M33 (Pinwheel Galaxy)
M34
M35
M37
M41
M42 (Orion Nebula)
M44
M46
M52
M57 (Ring Nebula)

M67
M92
M104 (Sombrero
  Galaxy)
Markab
Mars
Matar
Media
Menkalinan
Merak
Mercury
Merope (Pleiades)
Mesarthim
Mintaka
Mirach
Mirfak
Mirzam
Muphrid
Mizar
Nashira
Neptune
Nunki
Petra
Phecda
Pi Sagittarii
Pluto
Polaris
Pollux
Porrima
Procyon
Rasalhague
Rastaban
Regulus
Rosette Nebula
Ruchbah
Sabik
Sadalmelik
Sadalsud
Sadr
Saiph
Sargas
Saturn
Saturn Nebula
Scat
Scheat
Schedar
Shaula
Sheratin
Sigma Scorpii
Sirius
Spica
Tarazed

Tau Scorpii
Theta Aurigae
Tsih
Unuk
Vega
Venus
Vindemiatrix
Wei
Zeta Cygni
Zeta Perseii
Zeta Tauri
Zosma
Zubenelgenubi
Zubeneschamali

***Elements and Inert
  Gases***
Argon
Carbon Dioxide
Helium
Hydrogen
Krypton
Neon
Nitrogen
Oxygen
Ozone
Xenon

Over 150 combinations
are also available.

Glossary

Allopathic- Traditional Western medical science and practice.

Atlantis & Lemuria- Ancient civilizations that existed in the Atlantic and Pacific Oceans respectively, which were highly advanced spiritually and technologically.

Chakra- Energy centers that correspond to specific organs and endocrine glands which are located slightly outside of the physical body. Chakras regulate the energy and physical systems of the body.

Devic (Deva) Realm- Nature spirits existing in a different dimension and higher frequency, which oversee all aspects of nature.

Doctrine of Signatures- System of identifying the purpose and energetic functions of living things by their structure, form, color and aroma.

Dosage Dilution- Diluted stock essence, often given to animals and children, usually 4-7 drops of stock strength into 1 oz. alcohol water.

Electromagnetic Field Radiation (E.M.F.)- Toxic energetic pollution from power lines, radar and microwave towers, high-powered electrical appliances and computers.

Energetic Aromatherapy- The vibrational qualities and application of aromatic essential oils.

Energetic Resonance- The life process by which all living things radiate, attract, unify, and repel each other, particularly in regard to vibrational medicines.

Energetic System- The entire system of invisible subtle bodies which exist around and beyond the physical body, as well as the chakras and meridians.

Energetic Transference- The process by which the energy of the plant, gem, star or sacred site is transferred into water by the sun, moon, environmental condition or instrument.

Essential Oils- Not to be confused with vibrational remedies, pure essential oils are fragrant aromatherapy oils naturally distilled from flowers and plants.

Healing Crisis- A short-lived intensification of symptoms of illness that can occur as part of the healing process.

Holographic Imprint- Multi-dimensional form, wherein the whole exists in any of the parts. In the process of energetic transference, the energy is transferred wholly and multi-dimensionally, containing all aspects of the energy source, even in the smallest dilution.

Meridians- Energetic channels which run throughout the body, carrying subtle energy.

Mother Essence- Pure solar or lunar or starlight infused water solution, which carries the energetic imprint of the flower, gem, element or star, usually blended with equal parts alcohol.

Prana- Life energy or life force.

Speciest- The belief that the human species is superior to another.

Stock Dilution- The usual strength that is sold by essence companies, usually 4-7 drops of mother essence diluted in up to 1 oz. alcohol water.

Vibrational Medicine- Energetic therapies which balance, heal and accelerate consciousness by resonating and attracting high-energy frequency.

Bibliography

Andrews, T. *Animal-Speak*. St. Paul, Minn: Llewellyn, 1994.

_____ *How to Heal with Color*. St. Paul, Minn: Llewellyn, 1992.

Bach, E. *Heal Thyself*. Santa Fe, New Mexico: Sun Publishing, 1931.

Brennan, D.V.M., M.L. *The Natural Dog*. New York, N.Y: Plume, 1994.

Brodeur, P. *Currents of Death: Power Lines, Computer Terminals, and the Attempt to Cover Up Their Threat to Your Health*. Simon and Schuster, 1989.

Callahan, S. *Flower Essences for Animals*. Mt. Shasta, Ca: Sacred Spirit Publications, 1997.

_____. *Flower Essence Therapy for Animals*. Mt. Shasta, Ca: Sacred Spirit Publications, 1995.

Chase & Pawlik, *Trees for Healing*. North Hollywood, Ca: Newcastle Publishing Co., 1991.

Deiser, R. *Natural Health Care For Your Cat*. Hauppauge, N.Y.: Barrons, 1997.

Fischer-Rizzi. *Complete Aromatherapy Handbook*. New York: Sterling Publishing Co., 1990

Gardner, J. *Color and Crystals*. Freedom, Ca: The Crossing Press, 1988.

Gerber, R. *Vibrational Medicine*. Santa Fe, New Mexico: Bear & Co., 1998.

Gurudas. *Flower Essences and Vibrational Healing*. San Rafael, Ca: Cassandra Press, 1983.

_____. *Gem Elixirs and Vibrational Healing Vol. I*. San Rafael, Ca: Cassandra Press, 1985.

_____. *Gem Elixirs and Vibrational Healing Vol. II*. San Rafael, Ca: Cassandra Press, 1986.

Hall, M.P. *Paracelsus, His Mystical and Medical Philosophy*. Los Angeles, Ca: Philosophical Research Society, 1997.

_____. *The Inner Lives of Minerals, Plants and Animals*. Los Angeles, Ca: Philosophical Research Society, 1973.

Hogan, Metzger & Peterson. *Intimate Nature- The Bond Between Women and Animals*. New York: Fawcett Columbine, 1998

Johnson, S. *The Essence of Healing*. Homer, Alaska: Alaskan Flower Essence Project, 1996.

205

Kaminski and Katz, *Flower Essence Repertory*. Nevada City, Ca: Flower Essence Society, 1994.

Kemp, C.A. *Cactus and Company*. Tuscon, Az: Desert Alchemy, 1993.

Lane, *Sunset Western Garden Book*. Menlo Park, Ca: Lane Publishing, 1988.

Leadbeater, C.W. *The Chakras*. Wheaton, Il: Theosophical Publishing House, 1927.

Liberman, J. *Light, Medicine of the Future*. Santa Fe, N.M: Bear & Co., 1991.

Madeiros, P. *Hawaiian Tropical Flower Essences*. Kealakekua, HI: My Island Publishing, 1994.

Rael, J. *Being & Vibration*. Tulsa, OK: Council Oak Books, 1993.

Saint John of the Cross. *The Poems of St. John of the Cross*. New York, N.Y: New Directions, 1972.

Schwartz, C. *Four Paws, Five Directions*. Berkeley, Ca: Celestial Arts, 1996.

Sheehan, M. *A Guide to Green Hope Farm Flower Essences*. Meriden, N.H: Green Hope Farm, 1997.

Smulkis, M. & Rubenfeld, F. *Starlight Elixirs & Cosmic Vibrational Healing*. Great Britain: C. W. Daniel & Co., 1992.

Stein, D. *Natural Healing for Dogs and Cats*. Freedom, Ca: The Crossing Press, 1993.

_____. *The Women's Book of Healing*. St. Paul, Mn: Llewellyn Publications, 1991.

Stein, P. *Natural Health Care For Your Dog*. Hauppauge, New York: Barrons, 1997.

Steiner, R. *The Group Souls of Animals, Plants and Minerals*. Rudolph Steiner Press, 1908.

Thompkins, P. & C. Bird. *The Secret Life of Plants*. New York, N.Y: Avon Books, 1974.

Waite, A.E. *Hermetic and Alchemical Writings of Paracelsus*. Montana: Kissinger Publishing, 1910.

Whitaker and Adderly. *The Pain Relief Breakthrough, The Power of Magnets to Relieve*. New York: Plume,1999.

Worwood, V.A. *The Fragrant Heavens*. Novato, CA: New World Library, 1999.

Index

altar, 19
Andrews, Ted, 4
angels, 17-19, 27, 56, 166
animal communicator, 21
animal research, 4
Atlantis, 71, 97, 111, 203

Bach, Dr. Edward, xviii, 70-71
blueprint, astral (energetic), xx, 70
Burbank, Luther, 71

cancer, 4
Carver, George Washington, 71-72
chakras, 35-38, 48-50, 155-156, 164,
        169-170, 173-174, 203
channels, 21, 71
chlorine, unsafe in water, 9
cleansing the home with essences, 61
crystalline structure, 97

devas (devic realm), 61, 72, 166, 203
dinosaurs, 28
DNA (acceleration), 107

Earth
    animals attuned to, 98
    Chinese medicine element, 63, 65,
        68
    every creature on, 18
    FIR waves and the, 179
    frequency (stepping up), 27
    magnetic force within the, 177
    power spots of the, 173
    pulse of the, 26
    rocks that carry energy of, 174
    stewards of all life forms on, 25
    stress, 9-10

Earth *(continued)*
    toxic energy held in the, 172
    wisdom and intelligence of the, 17
electric blankets, hazards of, 172
essence preservation,
    alcohol, 70, 97
    shiso, 70
    vinegar, 70

fear
    and breakdown of the body, 7
    breeds hatred, 25
Feng Shui, 10

Hilarion, 18, 111
Hildegard of Bingen, 71

illness, effects of, 7
immune system, and stress, 6
indigenous people, 28, 71, 97
    See also Native Americans
infrasound, 168
intuition (deeper sensing), 53-54, 58

Kirlian photography, xvii

Lemuria, 71, 97, 203
light deprivation, 27, 32
    and pineal function, 164
livestock, 9, 24, 60, 157
love, 4, 6-8, 168
    unconditional, 16, 25

Mother Tincture (solution, essence),
        20, 97, 106, 204
music, 70, 158, 169-170
musical instruments, 169

207

About the Author

Since her early teens, Sage has pursued the study and understanding of consciousness through healing. During her adult life she has researched and practiced in alternative fields of medicine, using sound frequency and energy healing and incorporating the world of vibrational remedies in the early eighties.

Sage now lives in the Rocky Mountains of Colorado, where she worked for Pegasus Products, the producer of the most varied repertoire of vibrational remedies in the world, for several years, as well as making her own special tinctures. She has had her own practice in the energetic treatment of people and animals since the early nineties.

Sage welcomes any feedback on treatment of animals with vibrational healing modalities that you may have to share. Please contact her through Blue Dolphin.

Printed in the United States
23120LVS00003B/216